PRAISE FOR *PRACTITIONERS*

These are exciting times to be alive. Yes, there are complex controversies, intractable problems, depressing statistics, and plenty to be anxious about. But there are also creative voices seeking to bring a vital Christian faith to bear on these challenges—seeking to build innovative and authentic communities of Christ-centered practice. You'll hear some of these voices in these pages—and you'll be encouraged, as I was.

Brian McLaren
Pastor, Cedar Ridge Community Church
Author, *A New Kind of Christian* and *A Generous Orthodoxy*

Around the world, practitioners in the emerging church are having fruitful and productive dialogue about the future of our faith. This book brings together some of the best of that dialogue from some of the emerging church's most innovative practitioners. Like so many good books, this one will challenge, frustrate and provoke many readers; and, like all good books, it will produce even more fruitful dialogue.

Tony Jones
Author, The Sacred Way
Member, The Emergent-U.S. Coordinating Group

Real, passionate, at times arrogant and scathing—something you'd expect for these emerging conversants—*yet* thoughtful, honest, pastoral and committed to God's concern for people. I found this book to be one of the best of the genre in passionately describing what they are seeing and sensing, rather than simply telling everyone else how wrong they are. No matter what you think of these brethren, or about the movement itself, this book will draw you into the conversation—one that is for all of us.

Chap Clark, Ph.D.
Associate Professor of Youth, Family, and Culture
Fuller Theological Seminary

Lots of books these days talk about what's wrong with church and what leaders should be doing. *Practitioners* transcends that to talk about what creative, missional churches and leaders are, in fact, doing.

Kara Powell, Ph.D.
Executive Director, Center for Youth and Family Ministry
Fuller Theological Seminary

The best practitioners create dialogue-rich communities of learning and wonder where collective consideration leads to collective insight. This book captures that practice on paper. Enter the dialogue and become a better practitioner.

Dr. Dave Fleming
Author, *Leadership Wisdom from Unlikely Voices*

Too often a chasm exists in the church between the elegance of ideas and the realities of praxis. The validity of this book derives from the beauty and messiness of communal experiments in living the way of Jesus in the emerging world. Readers will be inspired by the creativity, risk-taking and thoughtful action of contributing authors—and compelled to live out their own stories with courage and imagination.

Mark A. Scandrette
President of ReIMAGINE!
Spiritual Teacher and Poet
Coauthor, *The Relevant Church*

Practitioners will set the curious mind racing as it reflects on Scripture and culture and life. There is dialogue, discussion and no lack of passion. Let it stretch your thinking.

Dave Roberts
Author, *Following Jesus*
Coauthor, *Red Moon Rising*

Practitioners asks many questions that people in the Church today are asking. In a different approach and without pretending to have all the answers, it sets out to explore the issues. While almost certainly you won't agree with everything said in *Practitioners*, it cannot fail to make you examine what you believe the role of the Church is in today's culture and why you believe it. Challenging.

Mike Pilavachi
Founder, Soul Survivor
Author, *For the Audience of One*

Jesus told stories of the Kingdom—of fields and feasts, of lost treasure and found sons, of God active among the everyday lives of people. *Practitioners* beats with the same missional heart. It's honest and real and passionate. It contains stories of God, active among the everyday lives of postmodern people.

Steve Taylor, Ph.D.
Lecturer and Senior Pastor, Opawa Baptist Church
Author, *The Out of Bounds Church*

Practitioners

Edited by Greg Russinger and Alex Field
Foreword by Erwin McManus

Regal

From Gospel Light
Ventura, California, U.S.A.

Published by Regal Books
From Gospel Light
Ventura, California, U.S.A.
Printed in the U.S.A.

Regal Books is a ministry of Gospel Light, a Christian publisher dedicated to serving the local church. We believe God's vision for Gospel Light is to provide church leaders with biblical, user-friendly materials that will help them evangelize, disciple and minister to children, youth and families.

It is our prayer that this Regal Book will help you discover biblical truth for your own life and help you meet the needs of others. May God richly bless you.

For a free catalog of resources from Regal Books/Gospel Light, please call your Christian supplier or contact us at 1-800-4GOSPEL *or* www.regalbooks.com.

Library of Congress Cataloging-in-Publication Data
Practitioners / edited by Greg Russinger & Alex Field; foreword by Erwin McManus.
p. cm.
ISBN 0-8307-3808-8 (trade paper)
1. Missions—Theory. 2. Evangelistic work. I. Russinger, Greg. II. Field, Alex.
BV2063.P68 2005
266—dc22

2005013569

Rights for publishing this book in other languages are contracted by Gospel Light Worldwide, the international nonprofit ministry of Gospel Light. Gospel Light Worldwide also provides publishing and technical assistance to international publishers dedicated to producing Sunday School and Vacation Bible School curricula and books in the languages of the world. For additional information, visit www.gospellightworldwide.org; write to Gospel Light Worldwide, P.O. Box 3875, Ventura, CA 93006; or send an e-mail to info@gospellightworldwide.org.

DEDICATION

To Tim Garrety, friend, father, husband, practitioner
March 5, 1972–April 20, 2005

Your leaving has interrupted our living, and yet
it's your living that awakens us to live a life worth leaving.

Contents

FOREWORD

Greg Russinger is one of God's most unique people. His own story is a gift to all who long for hope and need to see evidence of God's hand at work in present times. Greg's life is proof of God!

Over the years, Greg has joined us in L.A. at Mosaic, and we have crossed The Bridge into Ventura. What we found there was a kindred spirit of the barbarian tribes. Greg is real, passionate, optimistic, gritty, edgy, spiritual and, I must add, brilliant. His heart is fueled by the passion of Christ and focused by a passion for humanity.

Greg has something to say. He has a lot to teach. He is an endless well of experience and imagination. He is one of those rare people that the more you are around, the more you like him and respect him. I'm glad his voice is being introduced to the broader community of faith—it should ignite some interesting conversations.

That is exactly what Soliton has done for several years—brought unique voices together in conversation. I expect *Practitioners* to do the same. Here you find a mosaic of voices and perspectives exploring mysteries and imagining futures. Each brings his or her own uniqueness, while sharing a common heart. May we all run to the edges, while keeping Jesus at the center.

Chasing Daylight,

Erwin Raphael McManus
Lead Pastor of Mosaic, Los Angeles, CA
Author of *The Barbarian Way* and *An Unstoppable Force*

CONTRIBUTORS

Spencer Burke

A former pastor and accomplished photographer, Spencer Burke is the creator of THEOOZE.com; the founder of ETREK, a new educational alternative for the local church; and the author of *Making Sense of Church: Eavesdropping on Emerging Conversations about God, Community, and Culture.* Spencer is a well-known speaker and the host of Soularize: A Learning Party for IndieAllies—a national gathering of traditional and nontraditional theologians, church planters, community advocates, artists and musicians. He is also the cofounder of the Damah Film Festival, an annual competition celebrating spiritual experiences in film. Spencer is married to Lisa, and they live in a small 1920s beach shack in Newport Beach, California. They have two children, Alden and Grace.

Craig Detweiler

Craig Detweiler is an associate professor and the chair of Mass Communications at Biola University. He is also a screenwriter and the author of the book *A Matrix of Meanings: Finding God in Pop Culture.* He wrote the films *The Duke* for Buena Vista (Disney) and *Extreme Days* for Providence Entertainment. His documentary *Williams Syndrome: A Highly Musical Species* won a Cine Golden Eagle and the Crystal Heart Award at the Heartland Film Festival. Craig serves as executive producer of the City of the Angels Film Festival and on the advisory boards for Reel Spirituality and the Heartland Film Festival. Craig has a master of fine arts from the University of Southern California's School of Cinema/TV and a masters of divinity from Fuller Theological Seminary. He is also a contributing editor for *Mars Hill Review.* He lives in Southern California with his wife and two children.

Tim Garrety

Tim Garrety was the co-owner of the world-renowned Skate Street Skatepark and the owner and operator of Foreword Media, a video production and design firm. Garrety was also the creative director at The Bridge Community.

Pete Greig

Pete Greig is the author of four books including *Red Moon Rising* and *The Vision and the Vow*. He invests the majority of his time into 24-7 Prayer, the missions and justice community he cofounded in 2000, which has spread into 58 countries. Greig is a theology graduate with a background in church planting and a commitment to the emerging culture. He currently resides in Chichester, England, with his wife and two young sons, and from this base they facilitate a learning community called *Transit* and travel all over the world.

Joyce Heron

Joyce Heron, the director of Jacob's Well in Vancouver, Canada, invests herself in teaching both locally and internationally. Through teaching and modeling God's heart for the poor, Jacob's Well seeks to allow others to discover ways in which they can engage with the marginalized people around them. Joyce's passion is to awaken and equip the Church to faithfully participate in God's mandate to love marginalized people. She can be reached at info@jacobwell.ca.

Dan Kimball

Dan Kimball is the founding pastor of Vintage Faith Church in Santa Cruz, California. He is the author of both *The Emerging Church* and *Emerging Worship* and speaks extensively around the country. Dan also serves on the Emergent board and has received a bachelor's degree in Architecture from Colorado State University, a graduate certificate in Bible from Multnomah Bible College and a master's degree from Western Seminary. He is married to Becky, and they have two daughters, Katie and Claire.

Doug Pagitt

Doug Pagitt is pastor of Solomon's Porch, a holistic, missional, Christian community in Minneapolis, Minnesota. He's also serves on the Emergent board and speaks all around the world. He is the author of *Reimagining Spiritual Formation* and the forthcoming *Beyond Preaching*. Doug and his wife, Shelley, are the parents of four children.

Anna Pelkey

Anna Pelkey is a visual artist who resides in Ventura, California. Her works of art—predominantly sculptures, paintings and drawings—emote a sense of wonder and story. Her sculptures are often made from wire and objects that she finds. Anna earned her bachelor of arts from Biola University and her master of fine arts from California State University, Northridge. She is a part of The Bridge Community, where she coordinates fine arts as well as the Render Gallery. The Render Gallery is an alternative artist space designed to exhibit artists' works in an unconventional environment that emphasizes experiential learning from both dialogue and visual communication. Anna's passion for her art, relationships and life all stem from the ever-encompassing love and intimacy of Christ.

David Ruis

David Ruis, along with his wife, Anita, has been involved with church planting and worship leading for many years. David's worship songs include "You're Worthy of My Praise," "Every Move I Make" and "Amen." He is the author of the book *The Worship God Is Seeking* and also lends his time to music production, songwriting and composition. David travels internationally, both speaking and leading worship across denominational lines. He lives with his wife and four children in Los Angeles, California.

INTRODUCTION

This is a quick warning before you get too deep into this book to get back out again. Maybe it would be better to consider this brief note, not entirely an introduction and rather than a warning, simply an informative gesture on our part; a reader's guide perhaps. You may choose to skip the following if you like.

This book consists of essays, dialogues and diversions, all of which came out of several events that occurred in September 2003 and 2004. These intimate little affairs, most often referred to as the Soliton Sessions, brought together a wide array of practitioners for incredibly rich discussion, dreaming, friendship, food, drink and otherwise unruly behavior.

Over the course of the next 250 pages, plus or minus (we will no doubt err on the 250-*plus* side), you will come across ideas in the form of conversations and dialogues that were written by various practitioners from around the world. The conversational chapters will be formatted appropriately, with little headings like this, "Monologue," or this, "Dialogue." You may also find other unique textual formations and narrative distractions jutting out of the primary story in wholly ridiculous places, and those may take on, but are not limited to, the headings "Story," "Blog Entry" and "Journal Entry."

You will *not* find definitions of certain words in the book, but our publisher suggested we provide you with several definitions. So here they are:

- *Missiology*—the study of the church's mission
- *Postmodern*—of, relating to, or being any of several movements (as in art, architecture, or literature) that are

reactions against the philosophy and practices of modern movements and are typically marked by revival of traditional elements and techniques

- *Sesquicarbonate*—a salt that is neither a simple normal carbonate nor a simple bicarbonate but often a combination of the two[1]

Bonus points go to the person who can find that last word in the book.

Some of the folks who responded to the ideas presented here have been dubbed, respectfully, Practitioner 1, Practitioner 2 and so on, in the order that they appear. We did this, essentially, because we didn't take down their names, and even if we had, it would have been too confusing for us, and for you, to try to keep track of the cast of characters that would have then populated the book. And as a result, this book might have read like a bad novel. But rest assured, everyone who participated was amply warned that we might deftly and accurately quote their ideas for the betterment of the book.

In all of this, we want to say that you should consider what you read to be, absolutely and totally, incomplete. We also tend to view the incompleteness of the book as a benefit rather than a detriment. By this we mean that the conversation is most definitely not over, and will be continued on the Soliton Network website, www.solitonnetwork.org, or the book's web site, www.practitionersbook.org.

Note: You may also stumble across discussions of issues that will unsettle you. And honestly, we're crossing our fingers that this will be the case. You will undoubtedly find yourself reading conversations that bring up ideas that will conflict with your own, as well as ideas that will invite you into the dreams of God. Through this introduction, we want to extend permission to wrestle through and even disagree with these ideas. We have observed of late a resistance to this kind of conflict in some circles of Christian faith, and you should know that we avoid that resistance, which is to say that we welcome conflict, questions and tension as critical sharpeners of our faith.

With all that said, there is little more to say. Onward.

Greg Russinger and Alex Field

www.practitionersbook.com
www.solitonnetwork.org

NOTE

1. *Merriam Webster's Collegiate Dictionary*, 11th ed., s.v. "missiology," "postmodern" and "sesquicarbonate."

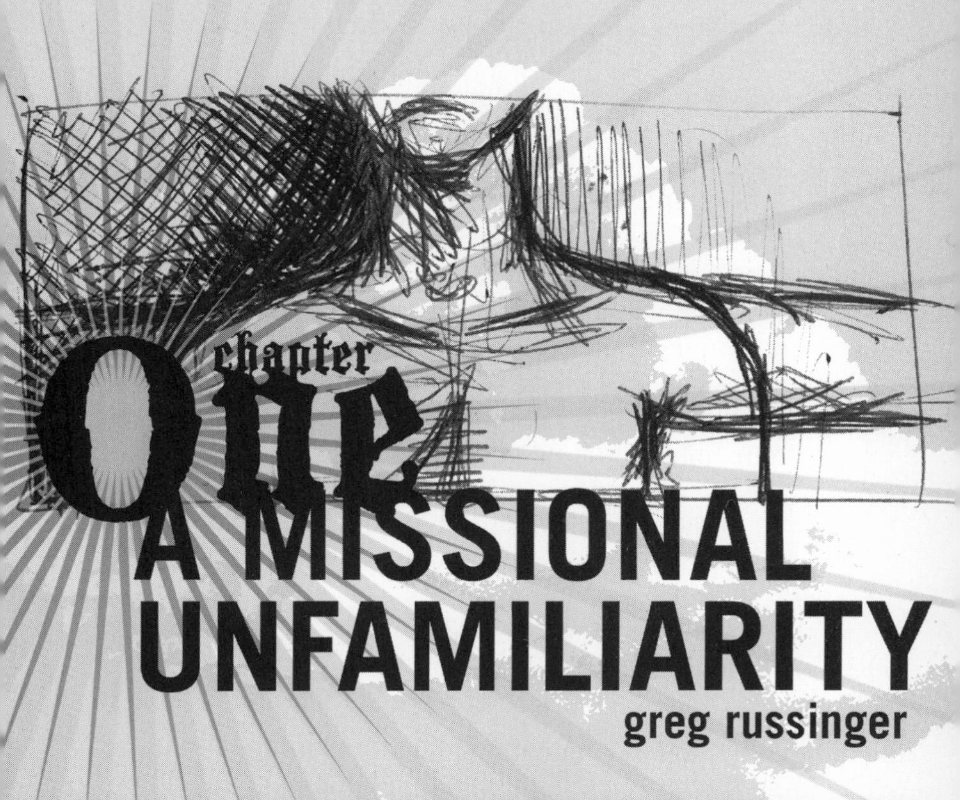

chapter one

A MISSIONAL UNFAMILIARITY

greg russinger

The whole conversation we're having in this book is layered with questions, curiosities and challenges concerning missiology and how we live as the Church. This layering of questions about who we are incites curiosity within "our" ministries and it challenges all the areas of life in which we serve, play, imagine, dream and walk.

In Jesus we understand the absolute depth of being missional. And for us as the Church, to look honestly into His face, to walk among His words and ways, to live within the skin of those He shared life with—friend, foe and stranger—these introduce us into the heartbeat of redemptive mission that resounds with a love like no other. A love so *generous* that it causes casualties within the control rooms of religious respectability. A love so *hospitable* that we wrestle with what it means to accept being accepted in Christ, because we focus too much on what we are not or on what people say we need to be. A love so *selfless* that those who walk in its depth, width and height shape a world through its secret humility.

A strong word of caution: This love, once flowing through your veins, may cause sudden moments of untamed unfamiliarity.

We all have different regions of life that we're very familiar with. You are familiar with specific people, specific noises, specific environments that you are exposed to on a regular basis. Most of us live within the regions of the familiar.

She mentioned

short indi[illegible]

for my [illegible]

are

now.

Cutting

away → carving

out something

new.

Nice, rang

true.

REFLECT

Write or draw below the places or people you are familiar with. Describe what makes them so familiar (their sounds, smells, regularities and so on).

In Mark 8, there's a story that deals with familiarity. I am often inspired by the questions of Christ and dumbfounded by His answers. This passage would read simply; but allowing ourselves to pause, we see a symbolic depth to the simplicity that demonstrates the ideas we're discussing in these pages. Mark 8:22 reads, "They came to Bethsaida, and some people brought a blind man and begged Jesus to touch him."

The friends of the blind man begged Jesus to heal his eyes. So Jesus took the blind man on an unfamiliar journey that caused some wrestling and reflection. First of all, we understand that for those who live within the dark realm of blindness, touch becomes the overriding sense that directs their lives; their fingers represent their eyes.

The many years that this blind man lived with his darkness forced him to learn to live in his familiar areas by touch and sound. He probably learned to get around in his own village and "felt" the familiarities within his environment. But when Jesus showed up that day in Bethsaida, a moment of uninvited unfamiliarity brought a blind man into the playing fields of the Christ heart.

Out of their friendship, those who brought the blind man to Jesus hoped for healing; their coming showed that they knew Jesus had removed blindness from others and that maybe their request would prompt the same. But when Jesus saw the blind man, He did something else first: "He took the blind man by the hand and led him outside the village" (Mark 8:23).

Why would Jesus lead the blind man outside of the village—especially when the village held the scent of familiarity for this man? Let's imagine this man's life for a moment: He woke every day knowing the sounds of the village, touching the architecture, stepping onto roads familiar to his feet, hearing the voices or laughter of neighbors, always being prepared to greet those who greeted him, smelling the scent of the marketplace as he passed through the daily routines of life. But on this day, Jesus decided to take him outside of this familiar village to lighten his dark world and maybe, just maybe, awaken him to the heartbeat of God.

In this unsettling yet hopeful moment, the blind man wondered what Jesus would do. He didn't have to wait long, for Jesus continued with a thrust of physical treatments from spit to touch. As this divine treatment began to take effect, Jesus asked a question that cries for our attention, just as it did the blind man's: "Do you see anything?" (Mark 8:23).

What a question to ask of a blind man who may not have seen anything for all of his days! The question lost its beat on the man's eardrums. It's a question that would be good for us to ask ourselves over the course of this book and as we live the ways of Jesus in our local context: *Do we see anything?*

Sight. As we swirl (sometimes blindly) through the rapid currents of cultural change, do we find ourselves clamoring for the anchor of familiarity? Though familiarity offers history and reassurance, do we as practitioners allow the unfamiliar to beckon, to call, to inspire us to dream the dreams of God in faith, hope and love? In the unfamiliar, we learn the tension and stress that say, "This feels so different that it seems almost threatening." For those who "see," for those who live in the familiar, it would seem implausible to venture out of the village. The village has provided a long memory of comfort and has become a haven of safety. The village has a clean scent, a flavor of routine that doesn't pull too heavily on the structures of our security or our theology. We have worked so hard at constructing the village of daily life that when the gentle hand of Jesus seeks to question our sight, how do we respond?

Maybe there are those around you who, like the friends of the blind man, so wish Jesus to lead them into the realms of the unfamiliar, who beg for healing to shape the present future of either personal or communal vision.

"Do you see anything?" Jesus asked.

The man looked up and said,

I SEE

PEOPLE.

[what does this mean?] journal your thoughts here.

I see people: This is the field where Christ plays. I see people: where justice isn't pop, but is the pulse of our local worship and global existence. I see people: where community isn't referenced, just lived. I see people: where inclusion and compassion are not some lifeless value statement, but a valve of the collective heart of the Church. I see people: where missional unfamiliarity is born and those infected live loudly through silent servitude and selflessness, which disarm the structures of evil. I see people: This is found as we gaze into the mirror, confessing we are God's beloved and then extending this love over spouse, child and neighbor. I see people: the unstoppable motion of God and His kingdom throughout creation.

My blog entry after seeing *The Village*, a film by M. Night Shyamalan

What does your village look like?
Is it that well founded, locked up, tight black boxes that sit
looming for young and unknown
to ponder its elements?
why the fear of the towns? After
all aren't they one big village,
keeping things locked and
undisturbed. they live from
difference and yet there
seems to be a universal fear of being. . . .
how long can one control the village?
or does the village control us?
how high can the secrets be stacked?
how daunting is life within the village
for those that walk with the skeletons of truth?
how the blind risk, how the blind see love,
how they live beyond fear, and reach
out their hands to succumb to trust. . . .
can we trust our village? can we costume our beliefs?
does nonexposure disorient the future?
or should we blindingly entrust the future to the
blind that see a future, hold fast to a future,
and journey into the future?
Love, its power to hope, to walk in and through
fear, its strength sustains when truth comes
out from hiding. Love sends and transcends. . . .
The village, a documentary, a commentary,
a philosophy, a psychology, a spirituality, or
just our humanity?

REFLECT

Watch the movie *The Village* and read Mark 8:22-26. Record your reactions in the following space.

SPOKEN WORD: LUKE 7:36-44
By Matt Gillespie

SIMON, *to himself*. I invite this much-heralded man, this man from Nazareth, into my home with all my friends. Is he that naive to what she is? Her lifestyle? Her sin? Or maybe he knows exactly who she is and allows this contempt anyway. If he was a prophet, he'd know. And even though he clearly isn't, he should still be able to see. I mean, look at her coming in here and trying to cover up her vulgar stench with the fragrance of perfume. She has done nothing good her whole life. I can't believe I almost fell into believing that this fraud could actually be the One. I am glad that this happened sooner rather than later. I wish she'd stop already. Enough with this disgusting display; this is embarrassing for my guests, and I'm going to put an end to this.

JESUS. Simon, I have something to say to you.

SIMON. Tell me, teacher.

JESUS. Do you see this woman?

SIMON. Yes.

JESUS. Two people were in debt to a certain creditor. One owed five hundred days' wages, and the other owed fifty. Since they were unable to repay the debt, he forgave it for both. Which one of them will love him more?

SIMON. The one with the larger debt cancelled, I suppose.

SIMON, *to himself*. Love him more? Here I have invited this man into my house, desiring that he would bring a teaching that imparted understanding, and I have been left with confusion. I am a teacher and a practitioner of God's law; I don't do confusion. It has been ingrained into every fiber of my consciousness that what is happening here is wrong. Yet my thoughts are obscured by this new and radical idealism. There's turmoil in my soul, but she seems to be free of turmoil. Is this safe? Is it right? How can I change who I am and what I know? I've invited him here into my home, and I know that I know better than he what's wrong and what's right. Don't I? Don't I see this woman?

HOSPITALITY OF SIGHT AND SIMPLICITY

We read the story of a woman who came uninvited to a dinner that was hosted by a man named Simon. Simon was a person of law in Jesus' day, a Pharisee, and he invited this teacher and prophet, Jesus, to dinner so that he could understand His ways. Jesus was probably at a symposium—a social gathering in which discussions of philosophy and religious ideas took place.

In the middle of this dinner, the woman entered through the door and came up behind Jesus, who was sitting there, probably in the middle of conversation. Then she knelt down and wept, her tears making a puddle next to His feet. She had been living some sort of destructive life—most writers and historians would say it was the life of prostitution. Overwhelmed by thankfulness mixed with shame, her body quivered as she rested at Jesus' feet. She had walked through the town to get to the place where Jesus was, carrying a jar of perfume with her all the way. When she finally found Jesus, she began to pour this perfume on His feet, and gradually the scent began to fill the room.

To inhale the scent of brokenness is free to all, for all carry deep within a jar waiting to be broken. This jar, entitled spiritual or human performance, seals up the perfume of honesty, transparency, vulnerability and forgiveness, preventing it from filling the rooms of churches and city streets. I long and live for a societal shift of transformative reconciliation under Grace, which unifies people to love and share without pretense or fear our common humanness, no matter how complex. I see the Christ practitioner as this Grace, led not by dogma but by a doxology of love that is heard throughout the earth; led by an emerging sound of selflessness sung down the boulevard of broken dreams, capturing the murmuring heartbeats of humanity and inviting them to join in the song that everyone can sing—you can hear it now—at the feet of Jesus.

All of Simon's guests were probably watching in a state of complete shock. And you can only imagine that Simon, the man of the law, the teacher, was sitting there, wondering to himself, *Who is this man? If He is a prophet and a teacher, why does He allow this woman to do this? She is known throughout the town as someone who performs acts of eroticism, so why would she bring this alabaster jar of perfume, which is worth so much and was most likely purchased out of her own earnings, pouring it on His feet?* It's funny how primal gratitude upsets the religious.

We can only imagine the silent disbelief that would have formed on the faces of those present as Jesus allowed this to happen. Blown away, Simon was probably wrestling with confusion, wondering why this was taking place in his moment, at his party, in his house, in his village—invading his familiarity, interrupting his church, rocking his theology, disrupting his philosophy and his upbringing. *Who allowed this woman entry*, he may have asked himself, *upsetting the worship, the preaching, ruining the order of service, making the church folk uncomfortable? Oh, that smell! Look at her clothing! I know who she is. Yes, she is that prostitute! Can't she control her brash display of emotion? This is unnerving. This is even hostile!*

And during all this, what did Jesus do (no bracelet waving please)? Jesus started a conversation as He saw the thought and intent of this man Simon, who was realizing the uncomfortable reality of what was happening, noticing the guests' eyes going back and forth in a nervous tick. Then Jesus spoke.

Jesus asked a question, another question for us to ponder as practitioners. But this question had a different slant from the one He asked the blind man. This time He asked,

"Do you see this woman?"

You've got to think that's a stupid question, Jesus. I mean, she's been sitting there for some time, Simon was probably thinking as he watched and pondered what was taking place, as he wrestled with the confusion of what he was seeing. And then Jesus asked the question,

"Do you see this woman?"

But what an epic question it was! And what a question He could ask all of us! Do we see that woman?

I truly believe missional living and cultural engagement find its shape in the posture of hospitality. Think about it: At one time, every friend that you have was a stranger. But how did you become friends? I'd like to propose that it was through hospitality. Hospitality primarily is the creation of a free space where the stranger can enter and become a friend. It is not about changing people, but rather about offering them the space of belonging and acceptance.

In their book *Radical Hospitality*, Father Daniel Homan and Lonni Collins write,

> Acceptance. Now there's a word loaded with meaning. We tend to confuse it with tolerance or even approval. But acceptance is about receiving, rather than judging. The father, who will not visit his son because his son is living unmarried with a woman, or even another man, might say he doesn't want to condone his son's choices. We feel for him, but we know it's a cover-up because we, too, have rationalized our avoidance of things and situations we would rather not have to face. Then we hide the disappointment, cover the anger, and justify the rejection. We struggle in our best efforts to hold back judgment and just accept. Acceptance is not about condoning; it is about embracing. When we accept, we take an open stance to the other person. It is more than pious tolerating them. We stand in the same space and appreciate who they are, right at this moment, and affirm the Sacred in them.[1]

A hospitable space is determined not by place or location but by practitioners—it is wherever practitioners roam. From Starbucks to the local pub, from shopping malls to skid row, from Nepal to the Netherlands, from the theaters to your own homes, practitioners live by the rhythms of hospitality. Hospitality is not something you do—it's someone you become.

Simon wanted to quickly dismiss this woman because, in his day, any woman whose touch fulfilled the pleasures of men was ostracized.

From Starbucks to the local pub, from shopping malls to skid row, practitioners live by the rhythms of hospitality.

In contrast, Jesus created space. He allowed this woman to *be*, without any judgment, without any conditions, without any confusion. He allowed this woman—He allows the stranger, you and me—to come and sit, knowing that His touch, truth, time and relentless tenderness transform the human heart.

The posture of Christ pushes us into a missiology of hospitality. As we read His story, we can hear hope, laughter and wholeness speak through the skin of those who encountered His redemptive hospitality.

This redemption cries for the Church to be the new urban monasteries, welcoming others into a hospitable collision with Christ and Cross. Let us live daily in the rhythms of Jesus, where moving over and experiencing the other, the stranger, become as natural as breathing. Though at first we sputter like a newborn gasping for air, through time, temperament and trust we foster this way of life that corresponds to the reply of the righteous, "When did we see you as a stranger and show you hospitality?" (see Matthew 25:38).

With this we undo the Christian notion that closeness with people is primarily a salvation cause mustered up by well-intentioned faith. We have learned to live by comic-strip thinking. In this comic, some "unsaved soul" stands next to us, and a thought bubble over our heads displays the mandate to lead this person through the Romans road and to pray a prayer, fill out a salvation card, go to church and become just like us! I realize that some who are reading this have encountered Christ that way, I being one of them. But after the fanfare and the rush of feeling and emotion of that moment are gone, what do we do then? For me, the people who shared in this occasion soon vanished, saying, "It's all done. It's eternal. Greg will do just fine." *My* spirituality became individual and I personalized salvation, leaving only a glossy grace, soon to fade without a communal exchange of faith, hope and love on this Emmaus transit.

Can you hear the sounds of the woman quivering at the feet of Jesus? Should we question why the religious didn't extend to her the unconditional warmth, reassurance and assistance of biblical community? In Jesus, we see the raw recognition of her human value come to the forefront and the rebellion of love challenge the systems of moral judgment that haunt the human heart, as well as confront church policy that unknowingly ousts the broken for fear that those with wealth would exit the doors.

May the hospitality of Jesus *pop* the comic-strip bubble that appears over our heads, curing us from the madness of methodologies that keep us outside looking in, dislodging our programs that taint the well (see John 4) and force love. May we be reminded that Jesus created space for people to be with Him, to learn from Him and to be loved by Him. Isn't it true that if Jesus abides within the fiber and framework of who you are, your invitation is to live alongside people in their spaces, for where you live Jesus lives. May people know Him because they know you.

Everywhere you place your feet the sacred lives. May the Church awaken to its creative and Kingdom intuition by being the space for others to belong, incarnating a hospitality in which belief becomes conversational and patient, not rushed and impersonal.

This woman experienced hospitality, not from the religious people, but from the guest of the religious people. This guest stands at the door and knocks.

the garden

A STORY OF HOSPITALITY AND HOPE

By Michel Cicero

The name "Jesus" did not slide easily off my tongue at the time I began to know Him. I believed in a Creator, but regarded Scripture with suspicion. My impression of Christians was less forgiving; I once attempted to sabotage a popular evangelist's crusade because I believed that his use of popular culture to attract youth was subversive.

Yet, like author Anne Lamott, I sensed Jesus around me, nudging, like a cat, long before I became His follower.

About a year before I really acknowledged Him, Jesus appeared to me on my living room blinds as I quietly ate lunch. He stayed there for a few minutes; and when He left, I missed Him. But I wasn't ready for Him. There were other signs—some blinking, some neon, some obscured by trees and buildings. One was disguised as a friend who went to a trendy church where everyone wore black and had tattoos. When I told him about my "sighting," I halfway expected him to convert me on the spot. Like Benny Hinn, he'd touch my forehead and I'd fall dramatically to the floor. Instead, he said, "Cool," and then lit a cigarette. There was something appealing about his underwhelm. His un-invitation was tempting, but still, I wasn't ready.

When I finally was, I decided to pitch my editor at the local alt-weekly newspaper a story about my friend's indie church. Under the auspices of reporting, I'd poke around but remain insulated from zealots and their attempts to save me. "Thanks, but no thanks. Just looking, not buying." I'd flash my press pass and all would be well.

Soon I found myself in the doorway of The Bridge Community with a curious expectancy, sensing divinity in the moment, the mystical touch of God's hand on my life, yet all the while denying it, pretending nothing more than a standard interview would transpire.

At first it was business as usual—introductions were made, polite small talk ensued, the tape recorder went on, questions were asked—but then I began to weep. Greg, the pastor, assured me that it was his black leather sofa and it happens to everyone, but I knew (and he must have known) that mountains were being moved.

I'm guessing some churches might have held my reluctance against me. The people of The Bridge Community welcomed it, and me. If I needed to sit in the foyer/gallery during the whole gathering because my tug o' war with God was making me anxious, they let me. If I didn't stand or sing during worship, no one seemed to notice. And when I asked if I could play in the dirt (the garden) in front of the building, they said, "Absolutely."

And so began my messy, beautiful, grueling and glorious accidental/on-purpose walk with Jesus Christ in, of all places, a church.

The soil was dry, rocky and polluted with chemicals. Whether or not it could support growth was questionable. On my first trip to the nursery, Dave, a man from The Bridge who had some gardening know-how, accompanied me. We met a few times; and given my intuitive approach to landscaping, it was a balanced, if short-lived, partnership. He'd mercifully dig the holes and I'd fill them. Together we'd water. There was some talk about God, but space was granted. Even when he warned me about "the enemy," he was careful.

The process of coming to faith was mentally taxing—no doubt at least partially due to my resistance—but I agreed to suspend my disbelief long enough for something to stick. The garden became my refuge, my expression, my rebellion and my surrender all at once. No one bothered me. No one directed me. I was unrestricted there in my own private Canaan. I had a place and I belonged there.

The long days of summer passed and the plants took root. Church became easier; people became tolerable; Jesus was becoming tangible. One night I was watching Christian television, when the televangelist du jour began to recite his version of the "sinner's prayer." I didn't know this was standard because I'd never heard it at The Bridge. I was feeling particularly receptive, as I was in pain from fibromyalgia and desperate for relief. I repeated the prayer and for reasons unknown launched into a dizzying confession. This was immediately followed by a vision: Jesus, lamp in hand (I had no biblical understanding of the lamp), knelt beside me, and His long hair brushed my cheek. Later Dave and I planted a papyrus plant; and now, when its silken pom-poms graze my face, I remember what Jesus told me that night.

In its first spring, the garden burst to life, seemingly while no one was looking. The soil teemed with worms and other insects. The papyrus was tall and muscular. One afternoon, as I knelt to connect the hose to the spigot, I spied something at once extraordinary and natural; new papyrus shoots had pushed their way through the mesh and mulch I had laid down to prevent weeds. It was a stunning testimony of hope. With unstoppable fury they'd pierced the womblike darkness of the dirt and reached hard for the light.

Nearly two years have passed since my interview with Greg. The story about The Bridge was published and the story continues. Eventually, I came to believe. There was no great revelation, no defining moment. It was more like an enormous exhalation. It was like a gentle loosening of my grip, the color slowly returning to my knuckles. Some days are intoxicating, fragrant. Others, arid and monochromatic. Few are lonely. And all are rich in possibility, like a blank page or an ugly patch of dirt that with care becomes hospitable.

THE SPACE TO DOUBT

On April 20, 2005, I arrived on the scene where my best friend, associate and partner in caring for the city of Ventura as well as in pastoring the community known as The Bridge lay lifeless on the street. How this image torments me every morning, how his voice causes my days to be slow and my heart to crawl closely to Grace. I now understand the love that David and Jonathan shared, a love beyond a woman's, a love bound not by words but by a friendship where life is lived for the other (see 2 Samuel 1:26). To say I miss Tim would be an understatement.

Through these fog-laden weeks I have come to learn the language of lament and have acquired a gratefulness for practitioners who are willing to sit in the dust with you and disregard the use of words *about* God. See, practitioners are those who know how to pain share; they know that being present is enough, that silence and servitude (without any God dialogue or declaration) can be healing in this journey through suffering. I acknowledge that wisdom needs its voice to speak and shape the future, but I agree with Walter Brueggemann, as he says, "The dispute concerns an unbearable mismatch between *lived reality* and *traditional explanations* that proceed by their own logic without reference to lived reality."[2]

My eyes have searched the story of God. They have feasted on the Psalms and have scavenged the city of Jerusalem in Lamentations; and yet, my rest and resolve are holding hands with Thomas.

In John 20, Thomas was the one disciple who hadn't seen Jesus resurrected. If I were him, I would've been pretty bummed. Everybody else had come back, shouting, "Hey, we saw Him! We saw Him!"

And Thomas was like, "Good for you." And then he said, "You know what? I'm just going to doubt it even happened. I just can't believe it. I didn't see it; you saw it. This is lame. I'm out; you're in—whatever."

The friends of Thomas, the disciples, had seen the resurrected Jesus—but not Thomas. His eyes were left starving for the joy that others had experienced.

Practitioners are willing to sit in the dust with you and disregard the use of words *about* God.

What followed? John 20:26 says that for eight days—for eight days—Thomas just hung out, wedged between life and doubt. This is a space where most people have traveled, a space where some are currently vacationing. In those eight days, Thomas mostly lived by memory, visited by the occasional neighbor of anger and pain. The loss of his friend of three years, plagued by the sounds of life continuing, probably pushed him deeper into the cold caverns of contemplation: *Should I leave? What would I do? Who am I to be without seeing my friend? Unless I see Him, I cannot, and will not, live; I'll just exist!*

And through this all, he was surrounded by the graciousness of space; though never alone, he could be honest with himself and others. He was loved. His doubt was accepted; it was never manipulated by the maneuvers of his friends or by impatience or intolerance. Rather, it was ingested into the very being of his friends, which shaped the space for Jesus to transform him.

Being practitioners of hospitality offers a subtle realization of how God works within the space of doubt, failure, pain and friendship. As Michael Card writes in his book *A Sacred Sorrow*,

> Your true friends will be willing to sit with you in silence not for a week, but for as long as it takes. Your real friends will encourage you to keep talking, crying out to, arguing with God. And when you would be tempted to despair and quit the dance floor, saying that you simply lack the strength or the faith to go on, it is only your real friends who will have the love to leave you all alone with the One who desires, above all, to finish the dance with you.[3]

HERE COMES THE KINGDOM

In Luke 3:7-9, John the Baptist tore into the crowd that went out to be baptized by him. "You brood of vipers! You this! You that!" John yelled at them. Then, in verse 10, the crowd raised a question: "What should we do then?"

John the Baptist, the forerunner of Christ (according to the prophetic utterance of Isaiah), the mouthpiece through which Christ's rule and reign would come, sat before hundreds and hundreds of people coming out to him to hear what they should do.

And here it is; here comes the Kingdom: "Hey, when you have two tunics, can you *share* one? And when you have some food, could you *share* some?"

"Excuse me?"

"Yeah, like when you have two of something, could you like *share* with the poor or just somebody who doesn't have enough; and if you have some food, could you make sure that you *share* some of that too?"

"So, you're the forerun—"

"Yeah, that's me."

The simplicity of the kingdom of heaven is found in this human tension—*sharing*. The missiology of hospitality creates space for people to see the Christ who knows us. The missiology of hospitality invites us to understand that the Kingdom perspective is as simple as *sharing*.

The future invites us to see—and when we begin to see the way Jesus sees, we engage in the human tension and the Kingdom responsibility of *sharing*.

NO LINES, ONLY OUR FEET

In closing, I share one of my favorite portions of Scripture, Luke 17:11. It says that Jesus was walking the border of Samaria and Galilee. This is a cool image. Samaritans were thought of as half-breeds and outcasts. And Jesus was walking with one foot in Galilee and one foot in Samaria.

Jesus knew no lines, only people. As practitioners, let us remember that there is no missional living without contact and that contact has been the activity of God throughout history.

Our whole conversation in this book will be a wrestling with the questions, the curiosities and the challenges. We don't want to wrestle in methodology or church-growth mechanics. We want to live dangerously and take advantage of the opportunity that the current cultural transition offers. Practitioners live a life where new discoveries, possibilities, hopes, dreams and friendships drive the language of a new missionality.

NOTES

1. Daniel Homan and Lonni Collins Pratt, *Radical Hospitality* (Brewster, MA: Paraclete Press, 2002), n.p.
2. Walter Brueggemann, *An Introduction to the Old Testament: The Canon and Christian Imagination* (Louisville, KY: Westminster John Knox Press, 2003), p. 295; emphasis added.
3. Michael Card, *A Sacred Sorrow* (Colorado Springs, CO: NavPress, 2005), n.p.

chapter 2

PETE GREIG

THE MISSIOLOGY OF PRAYER

With all prayer and petition pray at all times in the Spirit, and with this in view, be on the alert with all perseverance and petition for all the saints.
Ephesians 6:18, *NASB*

My name is Pete Greig, and I'm the completely bewildered person who finds himself one of the key catalysts within an international, interdenominational community called 24-7 Prayer, which started by accident in 1999. For 10 years I was involved in church planting, establishing two congregations focused on students in the emerging culture. We didn't really have the vocabulary nine years ago to be talking about missional communities, but that's really what we were trying to do.

We planted these churches in bars in the southeast of England. One of them grew and continues to be a very healthy expression of Christian community in the emerging culture. The other congregation went well at first, but then began to struggle because of some leadership problems and a deconstructionist approach, which we now realize was misguided. There was some great fruit from it, but the community has sadly dissipated.

Six years ago, my wife and I felt like it was time to pass the baton of leadership of these two congregations to others and to find out what was next. During that time I got kind of insecure. It's amazing how much of your identity can get wrapped up in what you do, no matter how hard you try to make sure that doesn't happen.

After several years of church planting, we realized that the congregations we had planted reflected our strengths and weaknesses: They were good at building relationships and community, good at celebrating and creating, and good at generating ideas; but they were terrible at praying. I am ashamed to admit that our public profile was outstripping our private spirituality. It was a guilty secret.

People were praising us publicly for our innovative and relational approach to church, while privately we weren't spending time doing the most basic disciplines, such as talking with God or sitting with our Bibles open and reading. This private hypocrisy was, of course, also reflected in our corporate times of prayer. Weekly prayer meetings were lonely little affairs, attended, it seemed, by two old ladies and a goat (and the goat wasn't particularly regular).

Around that time, God called my wife and me to go on a journey, literally as well as metaphorically, to discover more about prayer. We had no idea that God was about to hijack our lives. We just sensed a call to spend the summer in pilgrimage and assumed that this season of traveling, making friends and listening for His voice was merely a stopgap while we waited and wondered what was next. However this journey would change our lives. It began in us a process that has revolutionized our experience of the dynamics of prayer. Over the last five years, our understanding has shifted from the conventional perception of prayer as primarily a power source for ministry—something we do "to make stuff happen"—to a broader vision of prayer as a paradigm for mission as well.

My wife, Samie, and I strapped our 11-month-old baby in the back of our car and embarked on a grand tour of Europe. That summer we were free from the tyranny of a calendar, able to live in the sacrament of the present moment, a day at a time. We would just woke up each morning and discover what we were going to do that day.

EUROPE

Let me pause here to say a couple of things about Europe that relate directly to prayer and mission. Sadly, as you probably know, in terms of the secularization of society, the European continent is farther down the line than America. In his new book *The Cube and the Cathedral: Europe, America, and Politics Without God*, George Weigel argues that Europe's deepening spiritual crisis is a consequence of living on "the thin gruel of secular humanism that excludes transcendent reference points for cultural and political life."[1] In the wake of two world wars, the Cold War and the rise of pluralism, the majority of Europeans have simply stopped going to church, unwittingly abandoning the very Christian worldview, the transcendent reference points, that once held the continent together.

The church-attendance statistics among young Americans aren't that great either; but they're even worse, and they've been worse for even longer, in Europe. For Dr. Livingstone's generation, the great missional challenge was Africa. For William Carey's, it was India. For Hudson Taylor's, inland China. Few people realize that, in our generation, the Dark Continent is no longer Africa, Asia or South America. It is no longer even the countries running from North Africa into the Middle East (nicknamed the 10/40 Window), although the needs of this region are immense. The greatest missional challenge of our generation, I suggest, is Europe; and the new breed of leaders emerging around the world at this time has a vital part to play in the reevangelization of the Old World. You also have a great deal that can be learned from our tragic mistakes in Europe over the last 100 years.

However, Europe cannot be written off. Breathtaking revivals may be sweeping parts of Africa, Asia and Latin America, but the majority of the world's Christians still live in Europe. What's more, many of the greatest historical and theological resources in the world remain in Europe. All this makes it even more tragic that the European Church is in a state of freefall decline.

Because of this desperate situation, a number of things are happening. There's a lot of experimentalism and creativity in the Church with regard to mission, prayer, worship and art. Bishops in the Church of England who were opposed to new expressions of church just 10 years ago are now saying, "Please teach us what to do." You may have sung songs by British worship leaders like Matt Redman or Delirious. You may appreciate the teaching of great theologians like N.T. Wright, an Anglican bishop. You may have heard of the Alpha Course, which has introduced literally millions of people to Jesus. All of this good stuff flows, perhaps in part, from a certain spiritual desperation, but also from an inevitable distillation of talent in the European context. The people who choose to stay in church tend to be serious about what they believe because, if they didn't, it would be so easy to walk out the door.

THE DISCOVERY OF ZINZENDORF

Driving around Europe that summer, Samie and I found ourselves in the historic village of Herrnhut, in southeast Germany. During our visit, we learned that in the year 1700, a child by the name of Count Ludwig Nikolaus von Zinzendorf was born in that region. His father was a law lord in the Royal Court of Saxony; and as a member of the nobility, the young count was groomed from birth to follow in his father's footsteps.

Accordingly, Zinzendorf was sent off to tour the royal courts of Europe to complete his education and ideally to find himself a very influential, powerful wife.

On this tour Zinzendorf went to an art gallery in Dusseldorf, Germany, and was transfixed by the painting *Ecce Homo*. Beneath the portrait of Christ wearing the crown of thorns were inscribed the words "All this I did for you. What will you do for Me?" Looking at that painting, the young count had an encounter with God and pledged his life not to the prescribed conveyor belt of royal duties but to the service of the suffering Christ, whatever that might mean. I love the fact that it was through a piece of art hung in a secular place that he committed his life and his destiny to Jesus.

Zinzendorf was to become a preeminent example of the convergence between missiology and prayer. His life and community help us see that the two are actually inseparable.

Returning from his tour, Zinzendorf allowed some refugees from Moravia to establish a village on his land. They were fleeing the Counter-Reformation, having been bitterly persecuted for their beliefs in salvation by faith, the authority of Scripture and the priesthood of all believers.

These Bible-believing Christians built a village on Zinzendorf's land and named it Herrnhut, which means "the watch of the Lord." That was in 1722, but by 1727 they were almost ready to kill each other! Zinzendorf, aged 27, basically said, "Enough of this." He got them all together one day in a little church building in neighboring Berthelsdorf, and he challenged them to covenant themselves as a community to Christ. There were apologies and repentance.

Something extraordinary happened: The Moravians began to organize themselves to pray in a persevering, disciplined way; they prayed in shifts. Suddenly that entire village became a transformed community of prayer, a community experimenting with some radical models of social structure and of economics that were neither communist nor capitalist. They continually "kept watch" in this way for more than a hundred years. And there was undoubtedly a missional heartbeat to this extraordinary prayer meeting, because within five years the Moravians at Herrnhut had begun sending out missionaries—missionaries who catalyzed the great missions thrust of the Reformation. Luther's Reformation had arguably got the right theology into people's heads, but it hadn't galvanized their hearts to mission the way that this little prayer meeting in Herrnhut did.

A bunch of refugees and peasants had discovered the inherent missiology of prayer—the very dynamic that had given birth to the Church on the day of Pentecost. It was a simple, extraordinary model. They went out from that praying community in southeast Germany in pairs, traveling around the world to establish similar praying and witnessing communities. Moravians were the first to take the news of Jesus to the Inuit and to many other peoples.

As I found myself in Herrnhut, reflecting on all these things, this is what occurred to me: *I don't know what God's got for my future, but I do know that God's telling us back home to pray more. So if the Moravians could pray nonstop for a hundred years, maybe we should try a month of this nonstop-prayer thing and see what happens.*

LET'S GIVE IT A GO

Night-and-day prayer had seemed like such a great idea in Germany, but back home in England it seemed like a really bad idea. Especially when I worked out that there are approximately 720 hours in a single month. People at home were very sensibly saying to me, "Well, we're not getting anyone to come to any of our church prayer meetings—this is just stupid." In spite of such sensible counsel, we decided to give it a go, even if we didn't manage more than a few days of prayer. After all, we weren't trying to break any records—we were just trying to pray a bit more.

On September 5, 1999, a Sunday, we had our kickoff prayer meeting. I talked a little bit about the Moravians and Zinzendorf, and we prayed from about eight in the evening until midnight. It was just *really* hard work! We were trying to think of words to say to God. You can do that for half an hour—maybe an hour—but then the words just run out. I was thinking, *We've got to do this for a month. That's a lot of words we're going to have to find to say to God.*

Then at midnight we moved into a room that we had set aside as our prayer room. Some of the artists in the church had decorated it to be a creative space, a place that inspired us and made it easier to think. This way we didn't have to initiate everything. Over time, the images on the wall began provoking ideas that made prayer a reflex reaction. Suddenly prayer became a whole lot easier. People began signing up to do one- or even two-hour slots in the prayer room. One night, I went in at three in the morning, and there was just something powerful about the room. There was a vibe, a feeling—the presence of God—holy space.

More and more people started to experience that same sense of God's presence. All sorts of crazy things began to happen. People began to pray nonverbally, instinctively writing or drawing their prayers on the walls. One bloke walked in, gasped and said, "Oh, I saw this in a vision years ago. I saw this room with that globe in the middle and a candle, and people were praying. And the thing I never understood about it, and the reason I remember it now, is that there was graffiti all over the walls and the floor and the ceiling." We freaked out.

Spurgeon, the great Baptist preacher, said that people learn to pray *by praying*. Perhaps we need to read fewer books, go to fewer seminars and stop trying to get people to pray for our prayerlessness problem. Perhaps we just need to create a space for people to pray; to lock the door, throw away the key and see what happens next.

People were finding that God answers prayer. Who am I kidding? *I* was discovering that God answers prayer! I find great comfort in the apostle Thomas, because I'm not somebody who has ever found faith easy. I continue to question and default to doubt. Really incredible, incontrovertible answers to prayer began to happen, and I was there freaking out, shaking my head in amazement and whispering, "Wow! It's all true! Christianity, the whole Jesus thing—it really is true!"

I also found it very moving to see just how much pain is resident in a community of people at any given moment. There is always an aunt who is dying of cancer or a son who has fallen away from God and is doing drugs—there's so much pain.

At the end of the first month, we just couldn't stop. The momentum was too great. I would have been lynched if I had tried to terminate the prayer meeting! I couldn't believe that we'd prayed nonstop for a month. The second month went well, and then, in the third month, the movement just exploded. People started e-mailing and phoning us from various places, saying, "Hey, we want to open a prayer room to pray nonstop for a week or a month. How do you suggest we do it?" We wrote some suggestions on backs of envelopes and photocopied them and sent them out. We spent the first two years thinking that this movement was going to stop at any moment. But it still continues to grow and grow. In fact, it's growing faster than it ever has before.

So this explosion of prayer came and I was sitting in the middle of it, thinking, *This is bizarre, because prayer is the thing that we're bad at.*

24-7 MISSIOLOGY

Along the way a number of interesting things have happened. I have discovered that there is such a thing as a missiology of prayer, which is to say that you cannot divorce the intercessor from the evangelist and you can't divorce prayer from action. I'm suspicious of those who say, "Well, I'll do the intercession, and you go do the justice and service." I'm suspicious of that because we're all called to the priesthood.

I'm convinced that prayer needs a missiology as much as mission needs prayer. We've got to marry intercession with actual engagement and action. I don't see prayer primarily as something you shoot up to heaven so that an answer can then be beamed down to another place, although I do believe in miracles. I believe that the primary purpose of prayer is that we ourselves are transformed and become the answer to the prayer. In many ways, that is the most miraculous transformation of all.

The primary purpose of prayer is that we ourselves are transformed and become the answer to the prayer.

The baby boomers are so product driven that they have applied the same principle to prayer. They have seen it primarily as a way of getting something—be it money and a better house or social transformation and global revival. They have reduced the full menu of prayer to intercession and have lost the ancient traditions of contemplation, meditation and so forth.

These baby boomer Christians are now getting older. Many of them have been around charismatic circles since the beginning, and they wearily drag entire filing cabinets full of unfulfilled prophetic words around behind them, wondering how on earth so many things are going to happen in their few remaining years. All of this is creating a certain existential panic. Some are responding by becoming even more formulaic, deciding that the reason so many of their prayers have not been answered is that they've been praying the wrong way. They're becoming obsessively attached to some new idea about prayer that they consider to be "the right way" or a more effective way or a more biblical way. Inevitably, many of these "new ideas" are not new at all. They are old ideas, masquerading as new ideas, that surface in every generation. They are theories that get

or conceit,
but in others better than
yourselves look not only
to his own to the interests
of others. [5] among yourselves, in Christ Jesus,
who, though form of God,
did not God a thing
to be himself, taking
the form born in the
likeness being found in
human himself and be-
death on
a cross. highly
exalted him
which is above name, [10]
the name Jesus knee
in heaven on earth and under the earth,
[11] and tongue that
Christ is Lord, to the glory of God
8/2

preached with absolute conviction to insecure audiences—theories relating to the end times, the significance of the land of Israel and intergenerational or interdenominational Christian unity. The underlying assumption behind these theories is that there is simply some heavenly box that must be ticked, some giant revival switch waiting to be grasped in prayer. If we will pray in the right way, maybe the longings of a lifetime will miraculously be fulfilled in a matter of a few years.

Some baby-boomer prayer warriors have understandably resisted this "old formula, new formula" explanation of their own frustration. They have decided that they were simply wrong to put so much faith in the power of prayer and prophecy. These people have adopted a certain low-grade cynicism as a defense mechanism, a method of intellectual or emotional self-preservation against hopes raised and then deferred.

However, many more of these boomers are taking a middle road, neither hardening into formulaic faith equations nor softening into cynicism. These veteran Christians are realizing that when the apostle Paul advocated that we "pray in the Spirit on all occasions with all kinds of prayers" (Ephesians 6:18), he was implying that there are many ways of praying. These believers are finding great enrichment and an eternal perspective in the contemplative Christian traditions, which teach us how to pray in a deeper, more relational and less transactional way. These Christians still believe in miracles, but they stop seeing prayer primarily as a tool for productivity.

These Christians are also discovering that prayer must be holistic—interwoven into the fabric of our lives and communities. They are discovering that prayer is fulfilling and powerful when we stop *saying* prayers and start *being* them instead. We are learning that real prayer is incarnational and, therefore, inevitably missional.

MILLENNIUM 3 MONASTERIES

Eventually, we ended up starting monasteries. People began coming up to us and saying, "We want to go 24-7-365. We want to pray continually." That sent all my alarm bells ringing, as I thought, *This could just be the biggest Christian ghetto exercise. It would take a phenomenal amount of people's time and a phenomenal amount of resources to do something like this.*

When people started proposing 24-7-365 prayer, we said, "Okay, if you're going to do lots of praying in one place, in a monastery of sorts, could you please make sure that there's an art studio so people can pray nonverbally? Could you make sure you incorporate a ministry to the poor so that your prayers are actually heard by God [see Isaiah 58]? Could you please make sure that there's a strong missional dimension to what you're doing? And while you're at it, could you set up some accommodation where travelers and pilgrims can stay for a while and pray, as the monasteries of old once did?"

For us in Europe, the monastic community is a very strong metaphor and a good way of imagining what missional prayer might look like in practice. The Celtic Christian community called *muintir* was perhaps the most effective missional model that Northern Europe has ever witnessed. Many of our contemporary cities grew up around these abbeys or monasteries. At the heart of many of these economies, there was a house of missional prayer that offered schooling, medical care, lodging for travelers and some microindustry; it was a cultural center that also offered provision for the poor. It's very deep in our history, reflected in the layouts of towns, the names of streets and even the names of pubs. Seeking to draw from these ancient wells of missional prayer, we decided to call our millennium 3 monasteries "boiler rooms." Since the first boiler room, we've seen a number of them launch in the U.K., one in Canada and one in Kansas City.

The boiler-room initiative has been tougher than we ever imagined. But it's also been far more fruitful than we ever dreamed. We've seen so many people who wouldn't go anywhere near a church coming into these boiler rooms to genuinely pray, engaging with our prayer communities and even finding sanctuary when they are off their faces on drink or drugs. Once, our boiler room in Reading, near London, became the hiding place for a whole load of goths who were seeking to escape a violent riot. On another occasion a guy said, "Oh, you can really feel God in here, can't you?" This guy wasn't a Christian. I said, "Yes, you can, but you don't believe in God." He said, "No, I don't, but I can really feel Him here."

We've experienced the fact that people don't want to be preached at, but they still want to be prayed for. People who have struggled to have faith still somehow believe in prayer. Prayer is one of the untapped missional resources in a postmodern world.

MISSION FOCUS: IBIZA

Another more-intentionally missional dimension that's developed in this prayer movement is the crossing of cultural divides as pilgrim missionaries. We talk about the call to "pray, play and obey." We go to pray because we believe that there is something very powerful about "holy space" in an unholy place. But we don't just lock ourselves away in prayer. We also go to play, to genuinely celebrate the goodness of God in that place; this celebratory spirituality affirms the goodness of creation in spite of the Fall. Playing in a place might mean enjoying the beach, partying to great music, gasping at extraordinary sites and giving God credit for all the blessings we can find in the people and their culture. But if we merely prayed and played, we would fall short of truly missional prayer. Our prayers propel us into obedience. We seek to do whatever God tells us to do by way of living out our prayers on location. This often involves some kind of service project, relational outreach or another expression of justice.

A great example of this mission focus has occurred in Ibiza, a Spanish island in the Mediterranean Sea. Ibiza has some of the biggest nightclubs in the world and is the scene of fantastic music, deep wells of creativity and complete and utter hedonism. One of the biggest daily newspapers in the U.K. described Ibiza as the Sodom and Gomorrah of the modern era. Since seeing that headline, I'd been asking God for the chance to go to Sodom and Gomorrah to pray and see what happens. God answered that prayer when the churches on the island asked 24-7 Prayer to help them.

So we've been working there for the last few years. We've tried to put the tabernacle, or the place of prayer, right in the middle of the whole scene where the creativity is incredible. Privilege, the largest club in the world, is on Ibiza. It rises above the hills of San Rafael and looks like a spaceship. Inside there are pyrotechnics, palm-lined terraces, lounge areas and even DJs playing in the restrooms! There is amazing creativity and even community at a superficial level.

But there's also the really terrible side: The date-rape drug is everywhere. A lot of people who go to the island and are given this drug don't ever know that they've been raped. Every year many drunk people stagger down unlit roads and are killed by passing traffic. We can literally save lives by helping people find their way home. In Ibiza, missional prayer means clearing up puke, being sworn at, avoiding lecherous drunks and never ever leaving your water bottle unattended.

The wonderful thing is that, amid so much depravity, we're able to pray for people—that's our approach. Some of the guys on the Ibiza team are DJ's or bartenders in the clubs. They're not just Christians trying to access people from the opposite side of a cultural wall; they're actually living and working in the community.

We have also found ourselves picking up trash and syringes off the beaches. In fact, one summer we cleared an entire stretch of beach, but it took the whole summer. It wasn't a very long stretch of beach; it just happened to be incredibly trashed. Beforehand, the environment minister had told us, "We're hoping that if you clean it up, some of the species of animals will come back." So we were able to do this powerful, restorative environmental project as we prayed, played and obeyed.

It's very important to understand that picking up syringes from the sand is not a "good deed" so much as it is an act of prayer. For many years, Mother Teresa ministered to the dying in India as an act of worship because she had learned to find Christ in the poor. For us, the challenge of living prayerfully is that we somehow find Christ's face in a weeping drunk and advance His kingdom by filling a trash bag on a beach. This is the incarnational aspect of missional prayer.

All this may sound somewhat "worthy," when the reality is very unglamorous and often unrewarding. But now I deliberately want to tell you a miracle story to make very clear that I believe in the supernatural dimension of prayer, that missional prayer is not just another name for Christian humanism.

The Ibiza churches decided to do a big worship service with 24-7 Prayer at a nice New Zealand restaurant up in the hills. It was a wonderful time of great church unity, bringing together the island's gypsy, Spanish and Anglican churches. Near the end of the worship time, I said to the main priest, "Look, we want to be a blessing to you Christians on the island. How can the 24-7 community be a blessing to the Church?"

He said to me, "Well, I'd love it if you would pray that it would rain, because we're going through a major drought, and it's a real problem on Ibiza right now."

I thought, *Rats! I'm rubbish at prayer, and the idea of praying for rain is pretty scary.*

Without much faith, I said, "Okay, if that's what you want us to pray for"; so we asked God to make it rain. Then we got into our cars to drive home and as we did so, I remember seeing a single, unexpected splat of moisture on the windshield, as the first drops of rain started to fall. The windshield wipers soon started to churn months of dust off the windshield, creating the appearance of two arched windows. An unprecedented storm broke out and some of the guys climbed onto the roof of our villa to dance joyfully in the rain, worshiping God. It rained straight through the next couple of days. We later found out that it hadn't rained in July on Ibiza since 1976. The chances of such a rainstorm breaking at exactly the time we prayed after more than 20 years are slim indeed.

The BBC called me on the phone and asked rather cynically, "So you made it rain in Ibiza, huh?"

I replied without hesitation, "No."

"No? I've been told you made it rain," he said, nervous at losing a good story.

"No, no, no" I responded. "What happened is that we prayed. Then it rained. It's you who's making the connection."

"Yeah, but you were praying for it to rain?" he asked me.

"Yeah, but do you seriously believe our prayers could make it rain?"

He said, "Well—"

"Look," I said. "If you believe that there is a God and there is power in prayer, then maybe there was a connection. But if it's all just chance and we're just animals and the whole universe is just a chaotic, random mess, then let's face it, it probably was just coincidence."

Suddenly he blurted out, "No, no, no, mate. My mom's a Catholic. I think it probably was your prayers that made it rain."

And I replied, "Oh, thank you very much. That's very nice of you." The resulting story was titled "Ibiza: God Squad Claims First Miracle!"

It's truly amazing how much faith can be found in unbelievers when we stop acting pompous or trying to convince them of things. When we share our own inabilities and our own vulnerabilities with them, it's surprising how much faith we'll find that they actually have. When an airplane is about to go down, all the passengers suddenly discover that they have an extremely vibrant prayer life, without needing to resolve all their intellectual objections to God. At the heart of a missiology of prayer, then, is a profound awareness of the need inherent in all humanity, whether or not they call themselves Christians.

WHAT IS PRAYER?
Dialogue with Pete Greig

Pete: I've got a six-year-old kid from whom I've learned that sometimes the simplest question is the most profound. The first *simple* question I want us to look at is, What is prayer? Let's get a picture of our understanding of this word before we go any further.

Practitioner 1: Talking to God.

Pete: Talking to God. Are we happy with that as a total definition?

Practitioner 2: Not total.

Pete: Why are you not happy to stay there, to rest at such a simple definition?
Practitioner 2: Because God talks back. We move into conversation

with God, communication with God.

Pete: Okay, so it's conversation with God. I know this is Sunday School stuff, but bear with me.

Practitioner 3: I've started practicing silence as a way to pray; and in silence, there's a resting with God, being with God.

Pete: You know that Henri Nouwen points out that *hesychia*, the Greek word for "continual prayer," literally means "come to rest." So there's some relationship between continual prayer, which sounds exhausting, and coming to rest.

Practitioner 3: Is that why I fall asleep every time I pray?

Pete: Maybe! So how do you practice silence? No one is going to say that it's easy.

Practitioner 3: Honestly, I find that when I'm in a time of praise and worship and there's an awkward gap between the songs, I feel compelled to pray at those times. So I'm trying instead to just force myself to be okay with the silence rather than feel like I've got to start manufacturing words. Sometimes I do this in my car or in the mornings. Sometimes it feels like there needs to be some kind of communication between me and God, but I don't have words to say, so I just let the silence be enough.

Pete: Thank you. Anyone want to add anything to that?
Practitioner 4: I would say that it takes about an hour, or more, to shut down all of our busyness when we come before God. To shut

down all the lists and other stuff buzzing in our heads. But I still really have to battle through that hour and a half sometimes, because everything in me is resistant to that.

Pete: Are there times when we try to empty ourselves rather than taking those things that are filling our heads and using those in prayer? Does anyone here feel that we've got certain stereotypes of what God wants to talk to us about, or what time with God really looks like? That's not a loaded question. Do you have any thoughts?

Practitioner 5: Are you wondering what God wants from us in those times?

Pete: This aspiration toward a state in which we have emptied ourselves of the busyness makes me a little uneasy. It sounds very metaphysical and Eastern—not very Hebrew and earthy. It's important to quiet ourselves. But I'm wondering if you've got any thoughts about how we can actually take the head noise and use that in prayer, rather than try to get away from it.

Practitioner 6: I think, for myself, that I like to be doing something. For instance, I like to weave or draw a shape on my sketchbook, and I'll just cover the page with this one shape because there are so many things rushing around in my head. The repetition is soothing, so I find repetitions I can do to activate that part of my brain. It is really important for me to release something through my hands so that the rest of me can feel free to pray.

Pete: Thank you.
Practitioner 7: I've been reading some Henri Nouwen and trying to

A physical posture of humility can open the lines for us to see God's grace.

wrap my head around his talking about the idea of his whole life being prayer. I definitely don't understand that; I don't get that. To me, prayer is in those divine moments when we've had the hour and a half to debrief life and have come to a place where we can really listen. I've recently wanted to figure out what it really means to connect with God and to see prayer as that connection.

Practitioner 8: A couple thoughts that jump into my mind are the idea that we need to seek out prayer in a different way. Often we see prayer as a means to some other end. If I pray, then this will happen. Or if I say the right prayer, then I will connect with God—instead of seeing prayer itself as the connection. A biblical reference that comes to my mind is Hebrews 4, which talks about the invitation to labor to find rest. [It's] that place of tension in which you have to work, but it's from a place of rest that we pray. So Hebrews 4 then ends with [the idea that] now I'm just abandoned before the throne of grace. There's effort, but there isn't effort.

Pete: We also want to look at the different postures of prayer. Jesus literally painted a word picture, didn't He, in the parable of the Pharisee and the tax collector. In that story, the tax collector beat his breast and basically said, "I'm not worthy." The story actually makes a point of describing the postures. The Pharisee was standing and looking around, and the tax collector was kneeling and hiding. I think that [a] physical posture of humility can open the lines for us to see God's grace.

LIVING PRAYER

Now let's look at Ephesians 6:18. Paul had just told the Ephesian Christians to put on the armor of God. Then he wrote, "Pray in the Spirit on all occasions with all kinds of prayers and requests. With this in mind, be alert and always keep on praying for all the saints."

Notice the word "all." The direction is to pray on all occasions, using all kinds of prayers, and the implication is that there are many ways of doing prayer. We're also called to pray for all the saints. So we've got diversity here.

Let me give you something to hang these thoughts on. For me, the "all kinds of prayers" description refers to the upward, the inward and the outward kinds of prayer. The upward is petition; the inward is presence; and the outward is proclamation. There are the upward prayers of petition and intercession, such as "God, please change this situation!" Then there's the inward dynamic, which is the contemplative and meditative traditions of becoming the prayer. Outward prayer is the proclamation, the spiritual warfare, and I would bring into that the location in which we pray. There's something special about the place where we pray.

I'd like to focus now on the inward form of prayer. Many of us, especially those who grew up in a traditional Protestant context, weren't taught very much about this. That might be why people like Brennan Manning, Henri Nouwen and Brother Lawrence seem to offer a whole dimension of prayer that we don't get fed very much.

I had a pizza with Brennan Manning one time. If you're not familiar with him, he's a great writer who comes from a Catholic background. His life message is the grace of God. Anyway, I was just hitting him with all these questions about his life and he told me this great story. One time he was in a cave in the French or Spanish desert. There were a bunch of his fellow monks in other caves, in solitary, praying on their own for many weeks. They were mainly praying for this very simple village that was at the bottom of the mountain.

Imagining these monks praying for weeks in their caves, I just wanted to ask Brennan a bunch of really stupid questions, like "Where did you go to the bathroom? Where did you get your food? What did you pray about?" I think he thought that I was a bit dumb, but those are the things that I worry about.

At the end of several months of not talking to anyone but God, the tradition is that the village is so thankful to these men for their prayers that they throw a feast for them when they exit the caves. So all these holy men come out with big beards, like something out of a Monty Python show, and they proceed down to the bottom of the hill. Brennan admitted that he had been eagerly anticipating this feast for many weeks. The prospect of nice food and wine and music after all that time of asceticism and self-denial was glorious.

The monks got down to the village and found out that a bunch of students from Spain had come to visit their little monastery to get some kind of blessing from the holy men. Finding out that the men were not in the monastery but up in the caves, these students talked to some villagers who told them to wait a few days. The simple villagers were so excited to have these sophisticated students in their midst that they decided, *What the heck. Let's give them the feast.* So the students were honored by this grand feast intended for the monks.

The holy men came down from the mountain to find that their feast had been given to these young students who had ironically come seeking a blessing. What made it worse was that the students didn't realize that they had consumed the monks' feast and were so overjoyed to see the holy men that they decided to have a time of worship. They got out their tambourines and began dancing around the campfire and singing.

In the midst of this, Brennan found himself understandably struggling. Finally, the leader of their little community took them back to their little community house and asked to see them all straight away. "I watched you around the campfire, and I'm angry," he said. "Amidst the noise and the dancing, I could see that each one of you wanted to be back in your cave alone with God, didn't you?" Brennan said that they all nodded their heads. The leader continued with a profound observation: "God was no longer to be found in your cave. God was in the singing and the dancing and the noise and the offense. And if you didn't see that, then you didn't learn anything in all your time up in the cave."

God was no longer in the cave. He was in the dancing.

After telling me this story, Brennan turned to me in this pizza place and said one of the most profound things anyone has ever said to me: "God's name is I Am. He lives in the present tense. And if you do not meet with Him now, you will never meet with Him."

That to me is everything about what it means to practice the presence of God. As we grow in that, first we'll dare to meet Him in very obvious and easy environments, and then maybe we'll become like the true heroes of the faith, who can discover Christ even in a concentration camp or in an ER room when they're facing death—which each of us one day will.

As we sat in that pizza joint, Brennan turned to me and said, "Tell me something." He's from New York, and he's pretty forthright. "How do you know you've ever prayed enough?"

After a moment of fumbling around for an answer, I said to him, "Look, how do you see it?"

He said, "You know, those of us in the contemplative traditions believe that the most powerful thing that can happen in the place of

prayer is that you leave the place of prayer as the eyes and the hands and the feet of Jesus. I do believe that situations can change, but I believe the most incredible miracle that can happen is that you yourself become the prayer. And in that sense, what happens in what we traditionally call prayer is that we open ourselves to God so that we can live our entire lives as prayer."

Once again, I was kind of choking on my pizza thinking, *This guy is rewriting my understanding of prayer and perhaps even of faith.*

ON THE BOIL

Returning again to the boiler rooms that have 24-7-365 prayer, they really have strong community. I even had a guy from an organization that will remain nameless, say to me, "If you'll just call all these boiler rooms 'church plants,' we'll give you a load of money." Although he was a very nice guy, I didn't really want to do that. I just didn't want to get into that.

So I e-mailed him back with this reply: "The thing is, I might love your money, but let me just play devil's advocate with you. In boiler rooms people are meeting together daily, praying continually for the community and ministering to the needs of the poor. People are coming, beginning a journey with Jesus, continuing on their journey with Jesus. It does feel just a little bit like what happened in the book of Acts."

And he responded, "Yeah, but because you're not doing a Sunday meeting, it won't count as church for our donors."

So we had to say, "Well, bye-bye money."

If you look at the boiler room in Reading, you'll see at the heart of the community a core group of people who have built prayer into their lifestyle. For instance, an African guy comes every Saturday night and prays for several hours.

Around this praying core are all sorts of other people. Teenagers—just normal teenagers, who drink a lot of alcohol and smoke a lot of bad stuff and get into trouble—come to the venue. I could easily spiritualize this and say, "Oh, the Lord draws them." But the reality is that they come in because there are free Internet connections (and they really like the people). There was a period of time when every single Saturday, one of our guys in Reading would be down at the emergency room with one of these teenagers, phoning the parents and walking through that with them. Some of those teens have begun their journey of faith through that process.

I want to encourage you to mobilize prayer in your own life and in your community, both for the purpose of becoming an apostolic people and also for that of seeing prayer as intrinsic to your mission. We've found again and again that people who don't want to be preached at *do* want to be prayed for. In the wake of 9/11 and other massive tragedies, you've probably seen how many people will light candles, build shrines and even turn up at church. I'd love to see us having more and more places of prayer where people can instinctively go, whether or not they call themselves Christian, and know that they can actually communicate with God.

Missional prayer is about the two great adventures of life: First, it is about the inward journey of spiritual formation, learning to listen and to become the prayer. Second, it is about the outward journey of social transformation as we live lives of intercession, reconciliation, gospel proclamation and spiritual warfare. Missional prayer is like a highway—the traffic has to be able to flow in both directions. And when it does, when we learn to pray on all occasions, with all kinds of prayers for all the saints, we find that the kingdom of heaven is close at hand.

NOTE

1. George Weigel, *The Cube and the Cathedral: Europe, America, and Politics Without God* (New York: Basic Books, 2005), n.p.

chapter three

COLLABORATIVE VISUAL STORYTELLING

SPENCER BURKE, DOUG PAGITT, CRAIG DETWEILER, ANNA PELKEY AND TIM GARRETY

STORY
Monologue by Spencer Burke

To begin with, my hope is that those from the arts community will someday have a voice in the Church. Maybe now is our chance to start to share in story and metaphor and word and picture.

The Church is very literate, and I think that because of that, it doesn't understand "story" at all. I think the Church might have lost that power. So I'm fascinated when people talk about Jesus' parables or teach about Jesus' life, but miss the power of the words, the imagery, the *logos*, which is both word and image at the same time. You can't say that "logos" is one or the other, but because the printing press has ruled, we got the word. But "logos" essentially means image as well.

So I have this sense that there's something else that we can offer in this emerging dialogue, something that may not be captured or trapped by books. It may not be possible to capture this "something" in writing at all.

With that being said, I would also say that I am very concerned that *The Passion of the Christ* movie did so well and everybody's now ready to do a movie about the life of Moses. That's going to be dangerous, I think, because you're reducing the films that follow *The Passion*, which should be fluid conversations, to propaganda. Not art, but propaganda that simply brings the audience a movie, without dealing with redemption on a street level.

There's got to be something deeper, something more, in it. I'm afraid that the Church has forgotten how to even tell story, how to even engage in story, how to even listen to story apart from evangelistic skits or videos.

I come through the media-director's world. When I was a pastor of a megachurch, the first video projector I bought cost us $100,000. It took a crane to bring it into our church sanctuary. But it wasn't about story; it was about doing the commercial for the church's parking shuttle or doing the commercial for the women's retreat. We never did a 15-minute short film about redemption or pain or anger. And even if we had, if it would have had a cuss word in it or was somehow morally compromising or too realistic or dark in any way at all, it wouldn't have been Christian anymore.

So what I'm saying is that words can be part of this conversation, literal Scripture is part of it, pictures and story should be part of it, even commercials or propaganda can be a part of it; but not any one of these should rule the journey. My hope and my desire is that maybe we'll get good conversation started again with visuals and with visually oriented storytelling—because these good conversations got stuck, co-opted by money.

WHAT ARE YOUR THOUGHTS FROM WHAT YOU HAVE JUST READ?

Reflect in the space on the right.

STORY
Dialogue with Doug Pagitt, Spencer Burke and Craig Detweiler

Doug: Why do you think that certain versions of the Church, especially evangelical and conservative branches of the Church, have so avoided the issue of story? I have a suspicion that it's because our version of Christianity doesn't fit with the idea of story very well. And our problem isn't a method. A lot of the problem seems to be a message problem. In other words, it's not just the method of communication that doesn't work; it's also the very thing being suggested. Are there some broader reasons for why Christianity, across the board, has allowed preaching and telling a story, evangelism and everything else to be reduced down to a simple message?

Spencer: I would say that, in a sense, the commercial church has done that. But if you look around the world and see what's happening, I don't know that the whole Church got trapped in the same way. There have been beautiful storytellers, but I think they've been minimized. I think they've been put outside the Church in a way.

Doug: Why do you think that is?

Craig: My own theory is that it's a Protestant-Catholic rift. The roots of the Protestant Church are in icon smashing. We're iconoclasts by definition. We are an anti-image people. That's how we started. We took the art down, right? And we never put any of it back up. We just took it down. So our churches are all plain, with white walls, and a cross in the back. And it's a bare cross.

Doug: What caused Protestants to do that? Is there something in our DNA?

Craig: I think it's because we were founded on Solo Scriptura—that's our original tenet, which is chronologically tied in to the printing press—and the ability to disseminate Scripture arose at the same time that we took the icons down. Does that make sense? We have a good 1,500-year history that is Christian and artistic and visual, but we don't claim it as our history. We have to go back to that.

Practitioner 1: Some of us work in a church where Scripture is still, in a sense, the soloist. So when people start talking about this issue, they miss each other for really deep philosophical reasons. I know that most people don't like things that are petty, boring and theological. But if you run into members of a church leadership board who say, "Don't spend 12 minutes in the worship service running that film, because truth isn't found there," their understanding is that truth is found in the Scripture only when it's properly preached inside the worship setting.

Spencer: I agree. The problem is that in the previous 1,500 years, people also bought art. If you look at really bad Christian art, you'll see the faces of the friends and family of those who had money. If you look at the surroundings in the art pieces, you'll see that the artists took these subjects out of the cultural surroundings and put them into the surroundings that the subjects wanted Jesus to bless, whether it be a kingdom, if they had the money, or a rich family, to somehow justify their gluttony. So I think it got co-opted too.

Craig: But at least then it was pro-image. We're not even pro-image. We could be pro-image and make that art. But we're not even pro-image.

Spencer: I completely agree. And I guess what I'm saying is that I just would rather not have the pendulum swing back to prepress. I want to transcend that conversation and say, "Let's take the best of the premodern, let's take the best of the modern, and let's move forward." I don't want to throw out Scripture and I don't want to throw out imagery, but I don't like the gospel's being sold as four steps, where you can codify it.

ART IS DANGEROUS
Monologue by Anna Pelkey

True art and visual stories in general have often been viewed as dangerous. If you think about it, there are certain civilizations that we only know through their art, because that's all that's left. I think that when you take something like Jesus' story and make it into a film that has commercial value to it, then automatically you stamp it with a formula, and somehow you make the art safe. So we're doing this instead of saying, "Let's allow the artists to express themselves." That's also what happened when patrons asked artists for paintings that included Christ—they were making the art safe. In a sense, they were buying that artist and saying, "We want to make something under the guise of religiosity, but then we want to contain it. We want to control it."

Art is not about being safe; it's about being risky.

So they were buying the artist, and then they were dictating what the artist would do. And I think we still do that. I don't think it's any different with the art of Thomas Kinkade and art like his, even though we're okay with his. And those are safe.

Art is not safe, I don't think. I think that art, in a sense, is about being risky. So when we allow that to infiltrate the idea of God, it becomes scary. People fear that. When artists make images of Christ that are not traditional, people are afraid, not just of what other people will say or whether there will be misinterpretations, but also that an artist is going to say something wrong about God. So why don't we just stay where it's safe? But I don't think that is where we should be.

I think that risk is so important, and that is why silly things like tattoos are causing conversation. And to a certain degree, those

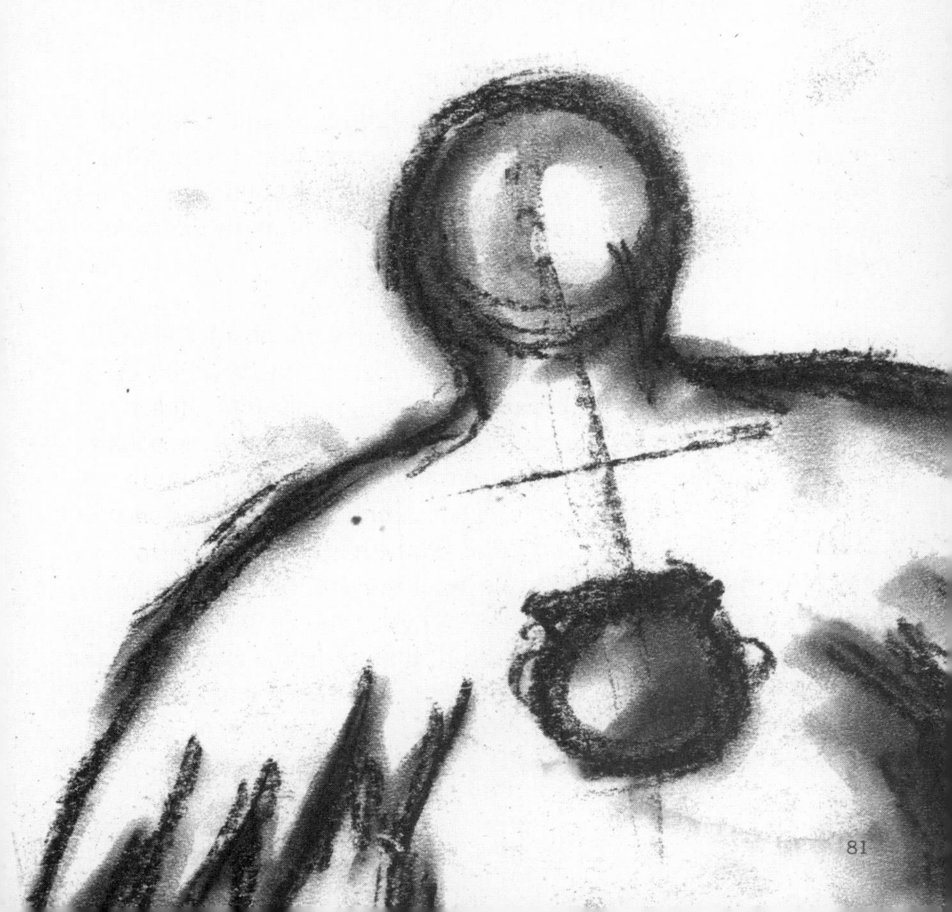

things are risky, though not so much anymore. I think that artists—at least the ones that I know in downtown Los Angeles who are not of the faith—are much riskier, and they're much more prone to be antagonistic, which isn't always a great thing either; but they're wanting to cause a disruption. That's what artists do a lot of times. And Christian artists shy away from that, and I think that's wrong.

ART IS DANGEROUS
Dialogue with Tim Garrety and Craig Detweiler

Tim: Something that struck me earlier is that, whether we realize it or not, we're saying, "We're willing to rediscover what Craig has exposed as a visual history that we've forgotten." So what is it that we—as spiritual people, as followers of Christ, as children of God—have lost at that point? What is it in our spirits, in our expression, that we're trying to regain?

Craig: I think that the beauty of metaphor and the beauty of open-ended story is the beauty of God. We've lost the mystery. Some people would say that words are more powerful, because the image is all in your head. Some would say that words give you more freedom. But I think more people today would say, "Just show me—don't tell me." And so we've been in the telling business, telling the story, rather than showing the story. When you were talking about the logos, I thought about Colossians, where it says that He's the image of the invisible God.

So we have to rediscover the truth that image isn't a reduction of God or a reduction of ideas or a reduction of spirituality. Image isn't an idol. Sometimes I can get more out of just spending an hour in an art gallery. I wouldn't know what God was going to do or say, but I knew that God would do more with me in that way.

Travis Reed, one of the creative minds behind Highway Video, has had no background in the Church, and I think that's why he's a great storyteller and an image maker—because he just came into it the way any person would, which is simply with the mind-set that says, "Hey, I'm just telling stories." And I think that's why he makes great little movies—because he doesn't care.

Practitioner 2: Craig, you said that because Travis doesn't have a background in the Church, you feel that he tells stories better.

Well, where I live in Tennessee, we all grew up in the Church. It's the Bible Belt, you know. All the leaders in my church have been in the church their whole lives. So it's so sad, but what you said is true: It seems as though people who have had a dramatic conversion experience, who have really experienced that journey from lost to found, often are the best storytellers. I think that the reason the Church is not good at telling stories is because we've not taught people that they have a powerful story to tell. Just because you've been a Christian your whole life doesn't mean you don't have a powerful story. That's something I struggle with a lot. I'm in a church full of people who don't really understand that idea.

So my struggle is this: How do I teach people that their story is just as important and it's just as beautiful?

Practitioner 3: Also, we don't often realize that our stories are connected to Martin Luther's story or Saint Francis's story. We don't always understand our communal story as the Body of Christ, or the history of the Church.

Tim: I think that even our view of Scripture suffers from that. We look at the Bible as stories, not as part of a bigger story that includes us.

STORY AND IDENTITY
Monologue by Tim Garrety

Spencer gave me an example of how he might walk anyone through helping them understand story. He simply asked a series of questions that could help somebody realize the stories inside of themselves. You are the story, from a scriptural perspective through what we retain of Christ within, but also through your experiences, your family or your life—no matter where you've come from, whether outside the Church or within.

So we walk around with this story. I think the reason that people outside the Church are better storytellers is because they find themselves in environments where their story is the most important, where their identity has been allowed to remain as a part of them, rather than in an environment where they've been disassociated with their identities and who they are. In the Church it seems like our identities cannot exist outside the presence of Christ. And so we feel this compulsion to just tell His story. So when we do a testimony, it's all about that point when I was saved. You don't really learn who I am just by hearing my testimony. You simply learn how I got to that single point in my life, and probably a little bit of where I've gone since then.

I think we're afraid of looking at who we truly are. That is the story.

REFLECT

What is your story? Write a whole story.

STORY AND EVANGELISM
Monologue by Spencer Burke

There's a classic scene in the movie *The Big Kahuna* where the two main characters really go after each other in their discussion of evangelism, and whether evangelism is simply the marketing of Jesus. I think that the difference between a sales pitch or a commercial for Jesus and true evangelism and relationship is the possibility of story. Think about Jesus: How often did He really even explain anything about the parables He told? To this day, we don't really know some of what He was talking about, but those stories were for those who have ears to hear. He didn't simply close the deal, He didn't say, "Okay, now we're going to have an altar call or now we're going to send out the sign-up e-mail list." He just didn't do those things. And yet, somehow the story kept going. Somehow it was alive and living, and the Spirit had more to do with closing the deal than human cleverness did.

Similar to the point of *The Big Kahuna*, I think that as soon as you put your hands on the story or the conversation and try to steer it, you have just stolen dignity from other people. You've just become Amway. You've just become kind of a multilevel-marketing game, in which somebody converted you, so now you're going to convert somebody else, because they're going to convert someone else and you'll be on the top of the pyramid. But it's got to be deeper than that.

So what I would ask is, Can the story be deeper than "I was lost and now I'm found"? You know, *Steel Magnolias* has a great story!

GET INVOLVED

Rent *The Big Kahuna* and share your thoughts on www.practitioners book.com.

STORY AND EVANGELISM
Dialogue by Doug Pagitt

Doug: We're in a tough spot in the Church when there's a sense that we want some sort of brand recognition for how good our product is. So if someone does a Christian film, there's this sense that it should now be packaged, put on a DVD, sold to a bunch of churches and made to compete with all the other general-market products. So I think that if we're really going to have that kind of conversation, we have to say that it doesn't have to be on a national or international scale.

Practitioner 4: I think we have to move away from competition and toward collaboration. I think in a shrink-wrapped, capitalistic world, it's all about competition. And scarcity is the mentality.

Practitioner 5: We live in a very image-based culture, and the image that's being promoted is very successful in influencing society in America. It appears to me that the image-based society that we have is also influencing the world at large. And the real question that comes to mind is, How do we tell the story of Christ through image in such a way that it doesn't leave everybody thinking that now they have to create some sort of beautiful image in order to connect with an image-based society? How do we manifest the story of Christ in images and visuals in such a way that people go away saying, "This connects with my poor state of being—my humanity"?

I'm not an artist. But I want to know how a story communicates to me the life and the beauty of the life of Christ.

THE PASSION OF THE CHRIST AND *FAHRENHEIT 9/11*
Monologue by Spencer Burke

The thing that I'm worried about is the fact that the two big films of 2004 were *The Passion of the Christ* and *Fahrenheit 9/11*. And what were they? They were basically two very extreme films. They were both promoted within these incestual little Petrie dishes, whether it was to liberal Democrats or to conservative Christians. What both these films tapped is the point here. *The Passion*, in the long run, probably didn't have that big of an effect because a lot of Christians were the ones who went to see it. *Fahrenheit 9/11* didn't have that big of an impact, at least not as big as the Republicans were all worried about, because it was a bunch of lean-hard liberals who went and saw it. It just proves one thing: that people will get really excited and spend a lot of money for *their thing*.

So I'm hoping that we move away from that and embrace broader films that help share the story. Why does it have to be a *Christian* film? I don't know if you saw it, but at the same exact time *The Passion* came out, a film called *In America* was playing. The *Christian Science Monitor* called me and asked me to go review *The Passion*. So I went and saw the film, and I said to the *Monitor*, "You know what? I saw *In America* the night before I saw *The Passion*. If I were to invite the people in my neighborhood to talk about the issue of redemption, I would invite them to *In America*. I mean, it's an amazing, powerful script."

The problem is that you never hear a pastor or anyone anywhere say, "I challenge all of you right now to go out to our information booth. We have *In America* tickets available. In fact, we rented the entire theater. We want you to bring your neighborhoods to see this film."

I think we need to start embracing films that might not be considered "Christian" a little bit more. We live in a Christian ghetto that says, "If they're not for us, they must be against us. Anybody who practices faith, meditation or prayer is evil if their focus isn't Jesus." Then we embrace criminals and crooks from the business world, bring them in and pay them high dollars to train our pastors to run churches as if the pastors were CEOs. And now some of these business crooks are in jail.

We need to start embracing films that might not be considered "Christian" a little bit more.

THE PASSION OF THE CHRIST AND *FAHRENHEIT 9/11*
Monologue by Craig Detweiler

I think Christians tend to look at film, art and really anything—even this chair—for utilitarian purposes. This *thing* is just a means to an end. This is a means to get the message out. Tolkien would say, "Don't do that to me. I'm not your means. I'm just telling the story here." I think we just have to think differently about art in general and art's role in a worship service. Personally, I think art's role is just to open people up, not to do the work that your proclamation is supposed to. Art is not there to deliver a message. It's there just to deliver a vibe, to sort of set a table for the Holy Spirit to enter into.

We love *The Passion of the Christ*. But a non-Christian is just like, "Man, this dude got killed! I've got no idea why." The film offers no explanation for why that happened. It's like a mystery story. There's no message in the movie, but Christians still say it has a message. *The Passion* doesn't really have a message. It's more of a tone piece. If you put on 85 minutes of that film, it's like, "Man, I feel sick to my stomach. Whoa! That was intense!" It creates a tone or a mood that opens you up, and then maybe you go, "God, what's going on here?" And then the Holy Spirit enters in.

THE VISUAL LANGUAGE
Monologue by Tim Garrety

One of the issues we can't ever get away from is the fact that we live in a culture that is very visual. We are taught visually and we learn visually, every moment of every day, every time we turn around. We even communicate using a visual language. The problem is that we understand a language that some of us don't necessarily speak. And as a result, we only get half the picture.

It behooves us, as carriers of the story of God, to begin to learn to speak the visual language. You don't give your life to God and become a Christian and then just come to church and listen to a message and get fed and never read your Bible. That just doesn't work. It's our responsibility to dive into God's story, allowing it to speak what it is and what He's trying to communicate to us. I think we carry the same responsibility to begin to learn to speak the visual language. Just as we read our Bibles and become more sensitive to the Holy Spirit's prodding, more sensitive to where the Holy Spirit would have us stop, we're going to be able to do that with a visual language in the same way.

Also, we can't ever divorce ourselves from the reality that we are directly responsible to God and for limitations He would impress upon our lives. But we do that too easily. We too easily want to say,

"Where is the line?" because we don't really want to think about it. We don't really want to learn the language; we just want to learn where the line is so that we don't cross it and so that we'll be good. We simply can't go through life that way. We can't go through life that jaded to our God, to the point that we don't want to be sensitive to how He might prod us one direction or another.

THE VISUAL LANGUAGE
Dialogue with Doug Pagitt and Craig Detweiler

Doug: I think part of the issue is that this is really new technology. A hundred years ago, people had never seen moving images before, but now we can create whole realities through film and sound. Back in the Church this shouldn't be something we wring our hands about. In some people's lifetime, this stuff is all brand-new. When you teach the history of film, it's a very new history. I think we should realize that it's going to take everybody a while to know what to do with this kind of technology. I think our nation is trying to figure out how to do that too.

It's not as though some people have this really clear idea of what to do with this medium. But we become changed people through watching film. I think the Church cannot have a conversation about that technology simply as technology, regardless of the message. There's missiological impact all over technology.

Practitioner 6: Do you guys all live in communities where you have these miraculous people who just embrace all, like you say, or are there stories of incredible friction, or have you been kicked out of churches?

Practitioner 7: In my church, people don't really like the idea of going to see R-rated movies. One of my pastors told me that he was going to take his two teenage boys to see the movie *About a Boy*, and I told him, "Well, you shouldn't take the children to see that. That movie has bad language in it." The pastor thought about this a second, and then he said to me, "I'll tell you what. I don't really care if my son says "F**k." I only care that he loves Jesus; and if he loves Jesus, he won't say "F**k." But I still don't know if that's necessarily something that I agree with.

Practitioner 8: That's a start right there. That's the gospel.

Practitioner 7: I don't know if I agree with that sentiment 100 percent, because I love Jesus and here I've just said those things.

Practitioner 9: More than once!

Craig: Can I give an anecdotal answer to your question? I run the film program at Biola University. We've got 200 students there who want to major in film. I've got another 200 who want in, but we've got no space for them. There are way too many kids who want to be filmmakers than we could ever teach right now.

These kids come in as freshman, and you could not find a more conservative audience to draw from. The first thing we ask them is "Hey, what are your favorite films? What are the films that have most impacted you?" They name films like *Requiem for a Dream*, *American Beauty*, *Magnolia*, *Fight Club* and *American History X*. And they say, "My parents don't even know I saw them." So the whole argument about whether cussing ruins a film's message is going to vanish. I think that very soon nobody's even going to know what that question means. It may have just tipped with *The Passion of the Christ*—because Christians just made an R-rated movie that grossed $350 million and more in the United States. That's the legacy we just created. Violence, we've never really been concerned that much about violence, because we're a violent people. Profanity will fall second, and then sex will be the last to go—or it may not go. I'm just saying that these things are going to be nonissues soon.

— lightley
padded
—padded
sewn or

POSTMODERNISM AND STORY
Monologue by Spencer Burke

From my perspective, I don't believe that we are just moving the organ out of the church and putting in the drum set. I don't think we're just moving the furniture in the Church. Fundamentally, we are at a crossroads in the Church at a massive level, and culturally we would call it postmodernism. It's essentially the idea of deconstructing, unpacking and reworking. It happened to literature and literary criticism in the 1940s and 1950s and is still happening; it started in our culture in the 1960s and continues; it began in business in the 1980s; and it's finally happening in the Church after the year 2000.

If you look at culture in the 1950s, McCarthy was in charge! If you questioned America, you were un-American, you were blacklisted, and you were not employable. You were probably jailed, if not even put to death; it was an amazing and strange time.

In the 1960s, just a few short years later, the very people who had been in power—in fact, they were at the zenith of their power toward the end—no longer even had any value to add to the cultural conversation. So then it became un-American *not* to question things.

In business in the 1980s, people literally believed that they would get a gold watch when they finished their long years with *the company*. They didn't have a problem with healthcare, because the company took care of its own. There was no such thing as downsizing. Maybe you did get a gold watch. The problem is that today, if you move from job to job (before it was seen as flighty, and you were a risk to employ), you're seen as a very well-rounded commodity. Do you see how radically that has shifted?

I don't believe that in the year 2010, we're going to be able to look back at the 1990s and even understand church. I didn't say the 1950s, and I didn't say the 1980s. Everything that we have as a resource today to tell us how to do church is like cultural

McCarthyism in a sense. The way that we're told the church should be done will be like the gold watch of the 1970s and 1980s—it will not work or make any sense to us in 2010.

So for me, I'm not often willing to gently say to people, "Oh, look, there's not a watch." They need to believe there's a watch. Still, I want to love, honor and respect them, because maybe they will get the watch, but we know that their kids won't. I'm not willing to live in that world anymore in the Church and listen to people who say, "So what do you do with a congregation?" You know what? I can't live there. I see the writing on the wall, and there are just too many people who are getting rejected, sprayed down by the Christian police and chased by dogs. There's just a little too much spiritual blacklisting, and I can't condone it.

I want to move out and find that artist, that visual storyteller, that person who's been disenfranchised, that person who feels that church has nothing to do with him or her, and say, "Hey, let's just gather around this table and talk about your dream. Let's help you find out who you are."

I think that in just 5 or 10 short years, we're going to look back and say, "Do you remember what we used to do in church? That was funny."

I truly don't think that this postmodern-church change is just a generational trend. I think it's fundamentally a shift, and I think visual storytellers will become—and I hope you take this the right way, because I don't believe in propaganda—the new theologians, the new apologetics experts, the new preachers. They will carry the Word into the new world in many ways. And it will be mysterious, and maybe it will be veiled. But God's Word will be living and active and sharper than any two-edged sword. It will touch people, but it probably won't be contained in the old worlds in which we thought truth resided.

WHAT WOULD YOU LIKE YOUR WORLD TO LOOK LIKE? Write it.

chapter *four*

MOVIES AND MISSIOLOGY

CRAIG DETWEILER

Martin Scorsese once said, "My whole life is movies and religion. That's it, nothing else."[1] To some degree, that's me as well.

I started out on my faith journey and came to faith because of movies. I remember when I saw *Raging Bull* as a high school senior. There was all this violent imagery on-screen, and I thought, *I'm kind of a raging bull myself*. Just like the boxer in *Raging Bull*, I had destroyed myself, my friends and my relationships.

When the Protestant Reformation came about, we took down the art, the sculpture, the stained glass and the paintings, and we threw them away.

The movie was two hours of sin and degradation—costly, ugly, self-destruction. And at the end of that two hours, the screen faded to black and said, "All I know is this: Once I was blind, but now I can see."

I had never experienced seeing before, but at the end of that two hours of blindness, I wanted to see. I think that movies, at their best, enable us to see in new ways. God reveals things in holy moments onscreen. We can't control God; He's bigger than all of that. If Yahweh can speak through donkeys, burning bushes and whirlwinds, then He can speak through Jim Carrey and the movies.

I want us to catch up with the things that I think God is doing through cinema. I believe that God is making a major move in Hollywood and around the world through filmmakers, artists and musicians, and we have the privilege of joining the conversation that God has started through these unlikely means. The question I want to ask you is, Has God ever spoken to you through a movie?

REFLECT

In the space provided, describe a film or several films through which God has spoken to you. Why did that film or those films move you?

GOD SPEAKS
Dialogue with Craig Detweiler

Craig: What movies have spoken to you?

Practitioners: *Schindler's List, The Matrix Revolutions, Magnolia, Signs, Lord of the Rings, Rabbit-Proof Fence, Saved!, Bruce Almighty, Braveheart, About a Boy, Gladiator, Lion King, Big Fish, City of God, Life Is Beautiful, The Mission, Les Misérables,* and *Eternal Sunshine of the Spotless Mind.*

HOW DO YOU THINK GOD SPEAKS TO YOU THROUGH MOVIES?

Craig: Whenever I get into a discussion like this, I wonder, *How does that happen? How can movies cause God to speak to you?* People's answers are always telling. Sometimes we see gospel truths manifested in the characters; sometimes we identify with the decisions the characters make, and we enter into their choices and struggles. A good film inspires us. Every so often, we'll see movies portray the truth of the human condition.

Practitioner 1: I like movies that heighten my awareness of my connection with the rest of the human race. It kind of wakes us up from the safe forgetfulness that pervades our culture.

Practitioner 2: I like to watch people who stand for what they believe in, which inspires me to say, "Why aren't I doing that?"

Practitioner 3: My favorite kind of movie is redemptive. That doesn't necessarily mean it has a happy ending. Redemption looks different for different people.

Practitioner 4: Sometimes I see a movie that gives voice to something that's deep inside of me that I was having a hard time putting words to. I think sometimes they remind us of traits or of things that we would want to have in our lives that aren't found in this day and age or in our culture.

Craig: Now look at this very short list of the qualities we love about movies. I hope that's what happens in our churches on a Sunday morning. Isn't that what we hope we're offering or embodying in worship and community? I think that movies, at their best, invite God into our lives and allow Him to show up in very powerful and surprising ways.

Also, I think that movies can effectively ask the right questions rather than give answers. Maybe that's why movies reveal truths that sneak up on us and seem to come out of nowhere. They create a space, sometimes a holy space, and they let you roam around in it. You get to find your place in that space and discover how you relate to the characters—who you want to connect with and who you want to reject, who looks like you and who doesn't look like you, who you like and who you don't like. Essentially, you see a mirror.

I think that movies are mirrors rather than morality makers, and those are two very different things.

CHRIST AND CULTURE

There is an Andre Crouch song called "Jesus Is the Answer for the World Today," which was a big hit in its day. Is this statement still true? Does it sound too simple or simplistic? Perhaps an updated, postmodern version of the song would instead be called "Jesus Is the Question for the World Today." Is that true? It's something we must consider.

Let's talk about *The Passion of the Christ*, the "little" independent film that turned into the controversial event of 2004. It put Jesus' life and death into public dialogue for a few months. Here's a quote I found in *LA Weekly*:

> More and more, Americans address huge social issues not on news shows, op-ed pages or the campaign trail, but through popular culture. . . . With *The Passion of the Christ*, our modern secular culture has bumped up against a homegrown explosion of fundamentalist belief. Where the Singaporeans and French confront such an issue by banning Muslim head scarves in public schools, Americans do it by talking about a motion picture.[2]

are shown
al order?!
ybe mother
in the midle?
Unless I
want more than
3.
more
dense
apron
w/ objects
more simplistic
Entrance b
Anex galle
cinderella
broom

Mel Gibson's devotional film generated massive controversy, and all the major news media tracked it. Everybody was talking about Jesus for a month. Cover stories asked the kinds of questions we as Christians would love to answer. What an opportunity! It does not get any better than that whole month leading into and coming after the release of the movie. Of course, *The Passion* was followed by another equally controversial film called *Fahrenheit 9/11*. The most surprising (and profitable) films of 2004 came from Mel Gibson and Michael Moore.

We can look at this and say, "Boy, they are two people who couldn't possibly have less in common." But what's interesting is that they both share the same religious heritage. In fact, after Michael Moore won his Oscar for *Bowling for Columbine*, he wrote a letter to the *Los Angeles Times* in which he apologized for giving an antiwar monologue from the stage. In the letter, he wrote that he had gone to church that Sunday morning of the Oscars, and when he was taking Mass and thinking about what was going on with the war in Iraq, he felt he just had to say something that night.

Both of these directors make films driven by their faith. Each man simply happens to express his Catholic faith in very different ways. Michael Moore's activism arises from a long Church tradition, just as Mel Gibson's conservative faith seeks to turn the Catholic Church back to pre-Vatican II traditions.

In fact, Catholic filmmakers are all over the list of the greatest filmmakers of all time. In a film history class, you will study directors like Alfred Hitchcock, who was raised in Jesuit school; and John Ford, the Irish Catholic who invented the Western. You will talk about Francis Ford Coppola, Martin Scorsese and Kevin Smith; and you will study one of the most popular filmmakers in history, Frank Capra, who was Catholic.

You cross over into Protestants, or evangelicals, and how long is your list of legendary filmmakers? Well, Wes Craven, the horror film director, went to Wheaton College. Paul Schrader, screenwriter of *Taxi Driver* and *Raging Bull,* graduated from Calvin College. Ron Shelton, writer and director of *Bull Durham* and *Tin Cup*, grew up within the Westmont College community. It's a comparatively short list.

I think that's because we have an anti-image heritage in the Protestant Church. We're anti-image and we're anti-icon. When the Protestant Reformation came about, we took down the art, the sculpture, the stained glass and the paintings, and we threw them away. We've got an anti-visual-art bias. We're promusic and prowords, and we've got all kinds of great Christian musicians and Christian writers as a result. We've got plenty of creative gifts within Protestant circles, but we've never gotten the affirmation to create visual splendor.

We need to reclaim some of those truths from our Catholic brothers and sisters and figure out how to reconnect with the profound heritage of Christian visual art. I believe that this will fuel our twenty-first-century filmmaking.

One good place to start is H. Richard Niebuhr's classic book *Christ and Culture.* It was written in 1951. In those days, nobody was talking about the word "culture"; it wasn't on anyone's radar screen. Niebuhr went through all of Christian history and basically said, "You know what, there are at least five biblical strands of faith. All of them have their own basis in the Bible, their own heritage and their different takes on how we should respond to God."

Each of the five strands of faith can be categorized by how it interacts with the culture around us:

1. "Christ Versus Culture" is just basic avoidance of culture. This is rooted in the distinct and passionate Anabaptist tradition. If you believe this is the best

option, you certainly won't go to see *The Matrix*. Why? Because it's a movie.

2. "Christ and Culture in Paradox" says essentially that you've got to be in the world but not of the world, so you gotta be cautious. What would this tradition arising from Lutheran roots do with a movie like *The Matrix*? That's where the R-rating question comes up. *What kind of content does it have?* you ask yourself. *It may be okay to watch, but I need to do some research first.*

3. "Christ Transforms Culture" says that you want to be in dialogue with the culture. Why would you go see *The Matrix*? In order to evangelize, to join the cultural conversation. You watch movies because other people are watching movies, and you want to be able to talk to other people about those movies in order to talk about your faith. This approach treats art simply as a means of communication.

These three options comprise most of the Protestant, evangelical response to the world and pop culture thus far. For the most part, our churches rotate among these three poles, moving from avoidance to skepticism to engagement (but only for the sake of evangelism). But Niebuhr observes two more options for Christians.

4. "Christ of Culture" is more like the Episcopal Church tradition that says, "Well, we'll just roll with whatever is going on in pop culture. We will appropriate what ever's going on in the culture and make it our own."

I'm not sure that's the best option, even though I'm currently Episcopalian.

5. The Catholic sacramental tradition is "Christ Above Culture," which says that God created the earth and all its little details, so I'm not going to worry about those. God is in charge of everything. I think this approach has an opportunity to say, "I go to the movies because God might be there, because God can genuinely be a part of the creative process."[3]

I don't go to the movie theater because somebody else needs me to tell him or her what a particular film meant. I go to the movies because I need to go to the movies, because God might be there, because God is a creative God. I think that difference in theology is what allows Catholics to make strong visual movies and Protestants to make talky, obvious movies, because we Protestants too often use movies as a means to an end.

HOLLYWOOD AND THE CHURCH

I have a drawing in which you can see Christian civilization at the top and the foundations of Christian civilization, which are the Church and the school, at the bottom. In the drawing, the foundations of Christian civilization are being attacked and torn down by modernism, denial of the Bible and Darwinism.

This drawing was done in 1922. Could something like this have been drawn today? A lot of people think that this is what we're still about in Christianity today. Now all they do is change the word "modernism" by adding "post" to the front of it. But it's still all the same stuff. It's still avoiding, and at the same time attacking, culture. You're going to get bad movies from that avoidance mind-set, and you're also not going to discover what God's doing in our culture at large.

This was the battle in 1922. Darwin was the enemy. Christians everywhere rallied to Dayton, Tennessee, for the big Scopes Monkey Trial, and they got beat—bad. Christians said, "All right, maybe the battle isn't over Darwinism. Maybe the moral decay in America is Hollywood's fault." So the Christian community went after movie stars like Fatty Arbuckle. Fatty got in trouble when he had a party in San Francisco and a woman died. Allegedly, he was making love to her, and he lived up to his name a little too well—she actually suffocated and died. He went to trial and almost went to jail. So before there was the O.J. Simpson trial, there was the Fatty Arbuckle trial. Christians jumped on this and said, "See, this is the problem! Holywood is undercutting the morality of America, so if we clean up Hollywood, then we'll clean up America!"

But Hollywood didn't really care, because business was good and sound recordings on film had just been invented. They had just done a movie called *The Jazz Singer*, the results of which were record-breaking box-office receipts. But then the Great Depression happened. It lasted longer than Hollywood expected. People still went to the movies to escape and see beautiful things, like Fred Astaire's dancing, but they attended in fewer and fewer numbers.

As the box-office numbers continued to fall, Hollywood said, "You know, this idea of cleaning up our movies, that's a good idea. If that will get Christians in the theaters, we'll clean ourselves up." In 1934, Hollywood agreed to adhere to a production code, crafted by Catholic priests and laymen. This sparked the Golden Age of Hollywood, when all the great movies that we measure ourselves by today were produced. These include *Mr. Smith Goes to Washington, The Grapes of Wrath* and *Casablanca.* This is the Hollywood that America loves and is trying to get back to.

This Golden Age continued right into the 1960s, when *The Sound of Music* and *Mary Poppins* came out—then whoa! What happened? R-rated movies appeared on the scene; and at that point, the old argument—it's all Hollywood's fault—returned. And we, as Christians, really haven't gotten away from that argument since.

In 1968, the Oscar for best picture went to *Oliver*, a musical based on a Dickens novel about an orphan scamp. There was singing and dancing; it was a G-rated movie for all ages and the best picture of 1968. In 1969, the Oscar winner for best picture was *Midnight Cowboy,* which was rated X. It dealt with male prostitution and heroin addiction in uncompromising detail. The huge difference between those two Oscar winners revealed the generation gap that was splitting America into rival camps.

Ever since, Hollywood has been viewed as a moral cesspool that Christians must try to clean up. But many of us were born after the *Midnight Cowboy* era; we don't know how to go back to an earlier time like the 1940s. We can't turn back the clock, because the only movies we know were made after *Easy Rider* and *Midnight Cowboy.*

OUR RESPONSE

How are we as Christians supposed to respond to so many voices, to so many messages, coming at us unfiltered? I can understand why we feel like getting in a bunker and just shutting them off. It's just an avalanche of information with so many conflicting messages that we couldn't possibly sort through it all. Thus were born the culture wars, the acting out of the avoidance mentality that we talked about.

But there are signs of hope bubbling up in independent cinema: Filmmakers like Wes Anderson and Sofia Coppola give me hope. And, of course, there's Quentin Tarantino, the king of independent cinema. Tarantino is probably the most hated and most loved filmmaker on the planet right now. You yourself probably have strong feelings about his aggressive, violent films. Very few people are neutral. His breakthrough film, *Pulp Fiction*, is one of the bloodiest movies ever made; paradoxically, it also happens to be driven by Scripture references and redemptive themes. Tarantino wraps the sacred in the profane. It's very confusing work. Where is God? Is God even in that? How can the sacred and the profane coexist in such a violent and entertaining package?

After sifting through all of this myself, I was still trying to figure out these questions: Why in the world would God speak to me through *Raging Bull*? Why not speak to me through a preacher? Why not through Billy Graham? Why would He do it through boxer Jake La Motta's beating his head against the wall? Why would God reveal the sacred to me through the profane? I didn't understand that. I needed some new theological categories, so a friend and I wrote a book called *A Matrix of Meanings: Finding God in Pop Culture*.

In the writing of the book, I took note of a few trends that I think are significant for Hollywood, for our faith and for our culture at large.

In 1999, *Entertainment Weekly* did a cover story entitled "1999: The Year That Changed Movies." Author Jeff Gordinier discussed some of the movies that came out that year, including *The Matrix, Magnolia, Fight Club* (the feel-good film of the year), *The Sixth Sense, Being John Malkovich, Dogma, Run Lola Run* and *American Beauty*.[4]

What common threads do you notice about these films? The article noted that these films have messed up narrative structure; the plots aren't linear; the editing is fast and choppy; the style is aggressive and in your face; the audience doesn't know who to cheer for. Gordinier declared that, in one year, the makers of these films completely reinvented cinema and the way we think about motion pictures.[5]

What *Entertainment Weekly* failed to see is what's going on in those movies. In every one of them, we can find something deeply spiritual at the core. Every one of them ponders and dissects the ultimate questions. Every one of them discusses the possibility of the supernatural breaking in: whether the movie be about God, forgiveness, doubt or frogs just up and raining from the sky. The films demand second viewings and postscreening discussion. They are packed with conflicting images.

In 1998, Mitchell Stephens wrote a book called *The Rise of the Image, the Fall of the Word.* As a Christian, I look at that title and I get a little nervous, because we're the "Word" people. So what am I going to do in this post-Christian, twenty-first-century, postmodern world that's almost entirely image driven?

In fact, Stephens says that the revolution has only barely begun. We're worried about a 500-channel universe, but it'll be 5,000 channels before long. Today we can carry around all our songs on our iPods. How cool is that? But in 5 years we'll have 5,000 movies on our iPods, and in 10 years every movie ever made.

So what are we going to do about this revolution? We can avoid it. We can try to filter it. We can say, "All right, I'm going to at least dialogue with it and maybe try to convert it." We can just throw our hands in the air and say, "I give up, because I can't resist it. MTV can teach my kids whatever it wants. I quit."

Or we can say, "Maybe God is up to something here."

Clearly, something is afoot when the best filmmakers on the planet, without getting together and having any conversations, suddenly think to themselves, *I'm interested in ultimate questions. I'm interested in how life works.*

That's when people of faith in the twenty-first century should start thinking, *What is the Holy Spirit up to?*

C. S. Lewis said it 50 years ago:

> The first demand any work of art makes on us is surrender. Look, listen, receive, get yourself out of the way. There's no good asking first whether the work before you deserves such a surrender, because until you have surrendered you cannot possibly find out.[6]

I find that God uses troubling movies to communicate to us and to make us ponder the big questions.

I think he's saying, "Give God a chance when you pick up that book, when you turn on that TV, when you enter that movie theater. Just give God space to work, because He's a big God and it's a big tent with lots of room for God to move."

Sometimes it takes so much work to get at the core of these films. Sometimes I don't have enough energy to dig deep enough. I'd rather have the simple Hollywood movie of old. Just give me an easy, feel-good movie. But I find that it's these troubling movies that God uses to communicate to us and to make us ponder the big questions. It's the complex movies, the tougher films, through which I hear God speaking.

PHILIP AND THE EUNUCH

There is a passage of Scripture I want to ponder for a moment. I've heard sermons about Paul at Mars Hill at least 18 times, and maybe you've heard that talk 18 times too. But nobody talks very much

about Philip, because he's mentioned only a few times in the Bible. But check out what happens in Acts 8:26-31:
Now an angel of the Lord said to Philip,

> "Go south to the road—the desert road—that goes down from Jerusalem to Gaza." So he started out, and on his way he met an Ethiopian eunuch, an important official in charge of all the treasury of Candace, queen of the Ethiopians. This man had gone to Jerusalem to worship, and on his way home was sitting in his chariot reading the book of Isaiah the prophet. The Spirit told Philip, "Go to that chariot and stay near it." Then Philip ran up to the chariot and heard the man reading Isaiah the prophet. "Do you understand what you are reading?" Philip asked. "How can I," he said, "unless someone explains it to me?" So he invited Philip to come up and sit with him.

The Ethiopian eunuch, referring to a specific passage in Isaiah, basically said to Philip, "Tell me please, who is the prophet talking about?" From there Philip goes deeper:

> Then Philip began with that very passage of Scripture and told him the good news about Jesus. As they traveled along the road, they came to some water and the eunuch said, "Look, here is water. Why shouldn't I be baptized?" And he gave orders to stop the chariot. Then both Philip and the eunuch went down into the water and Philip baptized him. When they came up out of the water, the Spirit of the Lord suddenly took Philip away, and the eunuch did not see him again, but went on his way rejoicing (Acts 8:35-39).

REFLECT

What does it mean to you to watch movies, engage with movies and talk to other people about movies—and what does it have to do with this passage in Acts 8?

Write down your thoughts in the space provided.

What's interesting is that we find this Ethiopian eunuch reading the prophet Isaiah, so clearly the guy was already on a spiritual search. He was on his way to worship a God he didn't fully comprehend.

What is our culture doing today? Are a lot of people sitting around in coffee shops reading the book of Isaiah? No, they're not. The Christians aren't doing that either. Biblical illiteracy is the norm in our culture; we're primarily viewers, not readers. So the spiritual search has shifted from looking at Scripture to looking everywhere else: movies, music, TV, celebrity, fame, sports—everywhere but the Bible. But the search is on nonetheless.

Do you understand what you're reading? That's the question that Philip asked the eunuch, and it's easy for us to ask the same question (adapted for our visual society): Do you understand what you're seeing in this movie? Do you understand Jesus? Do you understand God?

But we may not understand either. We may have seen the film *Donnie Darko* 10 times and still not be able to decipher it. So if someone asks us to explain where God is in it, I'm not sure we'd be able to. And you know what? That's okay! That's where the divine encounter can take place! We're there to dialogue and discover and have a spiritual conversation; we're there because we want to find God in that movie as well!

That's what I'm advocating here. Let's not come alongside just to buttonhole people with an argument and a bunch of answers. You don't go to see *Eternal Sunshine of the Spotless Mind* because you know that a lot of people will be interested in it. You go see it because *you're* interested in it. And if you're not interested in it, don't go. If it's not your kind of movie, stay home. But if you really love movies and want to join the conversation that God started, and if you want to be available to have a conversation like Philip's, you have got to figure out how to understand it as well.

To enter into that dialogue, you have to be willing to hear that person teach you what that movie means. *You* become a spiritual seeker alongside the person. And suddenly that person is telling you about how God is in that movie, and maybe you couldn't even see it for yourself. That happened to me when I saw *Memento* with a dear friend who is quite a thoughtful agnostic. I came out of the theater confused and angry. I felt that the director, Christopher Nolan, had played a trick on me, getting me to root for a villain. And my friend helped me realize the movie's brilliance and how closely it conformed to my own view of humanity. The level of self-deception in *Memento* is staggering. Our capacity to justify our most heinous action is endless. So after watching a dark film like *Memento*, I had the chance to talk with my friend about our capacity for self-deception and sin, which he brought up because of the movie.

Going back to that passage in Acts, it gets quite strange. When Philip and the eunuch came out of the water, the Spirit of the Lord took Philip away, and the eunuch did not see him again. What the heck does that mean? That's weird! Why did they put that in there? This would have been such a nice story if it had just said, "Yeah, he got baptized." But something freaky happened; the guy left and there's no explanation. Was he raptured? Did he die? Did the eunuch hold him under for too long? Was somebody drunk? As much as we would like to reduce the Bible to an easy set of answers, like the best movies, it still leaves me with questions.

IN CONCLUSION

Earlier in the chapter, I asked whether Jesus is the answer or the question. I think that with the coming of the postmodern shift, we have to discover that Jesus is actually a complex answer to very simple questions about the meaning of life, about where we find love, about where we find purpose. These are ancient, basic questions. And to say that Jesus is a simple answer to those questions might be too much of a reduction of His divinity and humanity, His mesmerizing Messiahship.

My faith journey has been complex. Jesus complicated my life when He entered it, and He hasn't uncomplicated it since. To me that's the postmodern shift. And I think movies at their best—the movies through which God speaks to us—are increasingly complex. They're increasingly troubling, and I think that God is actually increasingly present in that complexity— just like He's present in the troubling complexity of a book like Job, a book like Ecclesiastes or books like Psalms or Proverbs. The Proverbs seem simple until you try to live them out, and then it's completely troubling. God offers simple choices at the core of it. What happens if I do the right thing? What happens if I do the wrong thing? But in the real world, the applications, or answers, are very, very complex.

I appreciate the power of movies to dignify the questions, to wrestle with pat answers, to challenge the conventional wisdom. I am confident that God's truth can hold up to all kinds of scrutiny. But people of faith must be willing to enter into the unknown, to wander into a complex movie, confident that the Spirit will bring clarity, understanding and insight. We have an unprecedented opportunity to get in step with what God is already stirring up via movies, music and TV. May we all learn to look closer, to serve as faithful Philips, ready to engage with movies and their meanings.

NOTES

1. Martin Scorsese, quoted in Richard Blake, *Afterimage* (Chicago: Loyola Press, 2000), n.p.
2. John Powers, "The Ballad of Mel and Jesus," *LA Weekly*, February 27, 2004. http://www.laweekly.com/ink/04/14/on-powers.php (accessed May 31, 2005).
3. H. Richard Niebuhr, *Christ and Culture* (New York: Harper, 1951).
4. Jeff Gordinier, "1999: The Year That Changed Movies," *Entertainment Weekly*, November 26, 1999, p. 42.
5. Ibid.
6. C. S. Lewis, quoted in Craig Detweiler and Barry Taylor, *A Matrix of Meanings: Finding God in Pop Culture* (Grand Rapids, MI: Baker Academic, 2003), n.p.

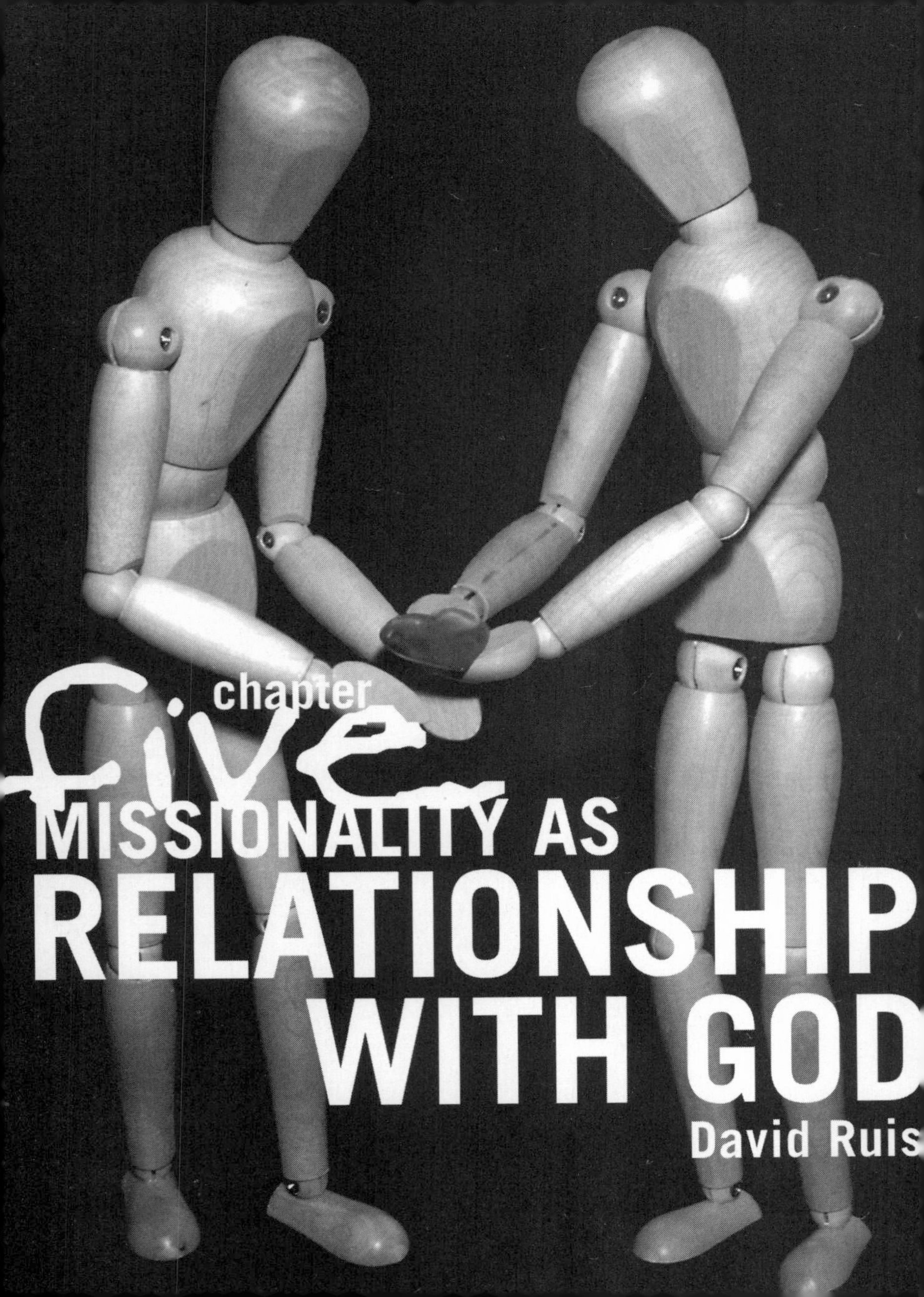

chapter five

MISSIONALITY AS RELATIONSHIP WITH GOD

David Ruis

In this chapter, we're going to wrestle with the whole concept of what it means to be a missional people. The logical place to begin the conversation is with the definition of the word "missional." What comes to mind when you say the word "missional"? What do you think about? How does the theme of being a missional people apply to your life and ministry? I've heard a lot of great responses.

Practitioner 1: To me it means to fit Christ and culture together in a way that makes sense in foreign lands and then to try to do it here at home; to learn from the old missionary tricks.

Practitioner 2: I think that being missional is joining God in what He's doing. Kind of giving God the priority and saying, "Okay, what are You doing now?" and allowing Him to shape your agenda, because your purpose is to further His purposes.

Practitioner 3: A lot of times, we think of the Great Commission, Matthew 28; but my perspective is that the missional mandate of the Church is to love God and to love our neighbors as ourselves; this is the starting point. And so in my mind, Matthew 22 always precedes Matthew 28. But a lot of times when we talk about being missional or doing evangelism, it's without dialogue about what it means to love God and to love our neighbors.

Practitioner 4: One of the things that I've heard about missional living that seems absent is the idea of Christians working together to reprioritize their lives instead of simply being missional as isolated individuals. The idea of missional community is important to me.

REFLECT

What does the word "missional" call to mind for you? Journal your thoughts below or go to www.practitionersbook.com and add more to this ongoing conversation.

GOD

I don't think God is static. One of the most fascinating Old Testament passages for me is Hosea 2. In that chapter, God had come to a place of absolute exasperation with the relational dynamic that He'd tried to create between Himself and humanity. He created mankind and yet also gave His people the ability to interact with Him or not to, to choose Him or not to.

This is one of the most stunning examples for me when I'm grappling with the character of God and the essence of God. We're talking about the only being in the whole universe who has the right—I mean if anyone has the right, God has the right—to demand obedience and complete subservience to His every demand or want or desire.

And yet He doesn't do it.

He leads in a completely upside-down way from the way that the systems and structures of all the ages teach us to lead. The mentoring of God is so different from how I approach the relational dynamic that I foster with people whom I'm taking on a mentoring journey.

I'm just so amazed by how secure God is. You know, in several of the psalms, we find the psalmist crying out thoughts like, "God! Vindicate Your name, for goodness' sake! People are slamming You! There are people who are completely botching up Your name. There are wrong perceptions of who You are everywhere."

These worshipful and intercessory heart cries are found throughout the book of Psalms and in other places of Scripture, and it almost seems as if God isn't quite as stressed out about the situation as we are. It reads like He's not motivated by stress or insecurity; He's not compelled to do what He does out of a need that He's trying to fulfill outside of Himself.

JESUS

Then we see missionality incarnated in Christ, and the concept becomes clearer. It becomes clear that Jesus is the exact representation of God. Sometimes we think in our heads, *Oh boy, if I could just see God.* Well, we do see Him in a very clear sense, in the pages of the Gospels and in the reflections of other biblical writers.

He's the exact representation of God, and here again we see this completely upside-down approach to the journey of the Kingdom. Jesus absolutely refused to let His disciples depend on Him. Have you ever noticed that? He rarely drew attention to Himself as a man. That's one of the tensions of the faith, you know—the goodness of Jesus and the humanity of Jesus.

There was an early heresy that swirled around the Early Church called Docetism. It was the idea that God simply couldn't take on a body. So there were all sorts of spiritualizations and wrestlings by which people tried to deal with the nature of God in Jesus Christ.

I've really come to the conviction that Christ fully took humanity on Himself. He didn't just wear it; He became it. He didn't just cloak Himself with humanness; He stepped into the entire depth of what it means to be human. I believe that Jesus learned, stretched, grew and wrestled with obedience. Hebrews 4:15 says that He even faced temptation.

So as a man that you could touch and smell and sit with and eat with and interact with and ask questions of, He constantly refused to have the disciples rely on Him. He always said things like, "I'm leading you to the Father," "I'm taking you to another place," "I'm giving you authority," "I'm giving you power."

One of the most stunning verses in Scripture is this: "Anyone who has faith in me will do what I have been doing. He will do even greater things than these" (John 14:12).

To me, that verse isn't about power; rather, it's one of the most awesome declarations a leader can make. Jesus wasn't here to prove anything. He was here to do what His Father does and, as He said in John 5, to invite us into that kind of partnership.

I see it modeled again and again in Jesus. He's constantly moving people toward the Father, toward the Father, toward the Father. There is this attitude of leaning into God and leaning into dependence on the Holy Spirit, which is absolutely critical in living life this side of heaven, this side of the return of Jesus Christ.

Jesus fascinates me because He was missional, because He truly interacted with people. Maybe that was the perceived blasphemy of Christ. Maybe that's what, in some ways, got Him stuck up on a cross. People might have said, "Oh, no, no, no! You can't be God. God doesn't have children jumping up and down on His lap and yanking on His beard and pulling His hair. No! God does not have prostitutes standing behind Him, weeping and touching Him and standing in His presence. No!"

It wasn't just the claim to be the Messiah and the One sent from God; it was His simple action. Many of the teachers and religious minds in the time of Christ had been raised on Scripture. They could quote long passages of Scripture without blinking. And yet there was God right before them in the flesh, and they couldn't see Him. They couldn't see Him!

See, I don't think we can understand the mission of God if we don't understand God Himself.

REALIGNMENT

In Hosea 2, we see that God was frustrated with His people. He was trying to move into this relational dynamic, and His people kept misunderstanding. They just kept trying to replace belief in the idols of the pagan nations around them with belief in God. Have you ever thought, *To follow Jesus Christ is to replace the other stuff at the top of my priority pile with God*?

I think that's helpful, but I don't think that's what God's after. He's after something that goes even beyond belief. James says that the demons believe and they tremble (see James 2:19). Does that mean that demons are better worshipers than we are? They have a clearer perception and awareness of God than we do. They believe and they tremble!

Philippians 2 makes it clear that before everything is said and done, no matter what philosophies and theologies we embrace on the journey toward the eternal moment of climax, there will be some discernible, observable moment when every knee bows and every tongue confesses that Jesus Christ is Lord. Can you imagine that?

Now for some people, it's going to be an absolute delight. For others, it's going to be the most terrifying thing they will ever have to do. The book of Revelation gives some potential insight into this moment. There's a passage that describes how, under the duress of this grand moment of revelation, some will call for the mountains to fall on them and crush them so that they can escape the encounter (see Revelation 6:16).

There will be this pressing of all of human history, of all the musings and creations of God, all being pressed toward this very narrow moment when every knee bows and every tongue confesses that Jesus is Lord. We will see Satan himself—at least this is my understanding of it—going down on his knee, saying, "Jesus is Lord!" I want a front-row seat for that, actually.

So in Hosea 2, God's frustrated and angry. I don't know if God can pace, but in my head, I see Him pacing around the throne room of heaven. I mean, just look at a few verses here.

> So now I will expose her lewdness before the eyes of her lovers; no one will take her out of my hands. I will stop all her celebrations: her yearly festivals, her New Moons, her Sabbath days—all her appointed feasts (vv. 10-11).

Basically, God's saying, "I'm going to crash the party. I'm going to come in and rip everything apart."

What is this? Is this how He feels? Is this prophecy?

As I wrestle with passages like this, I feel like I'm getting to see a small part of the heart of God. Clearly, He really cares about this stuff.

But what happens? Verse 14 is the big turning point. All of what God's feeling in verse 10, all of His anger and all of His frustration, is going to be manifested among us. And this is how:

> Therefore I am now going to allure her; I will lead her into the desert and speak tenderly to her.

Who is God to turn about like this? Who thinks like this? Who leads like this?

> There I will give her back her vineyards, and will make the Valley of Achor [or the place of trouble] a door of hope. There she will sing as in the days of her youth, as in the day she came up out of Egypt. "In that day," declares the Lord, "you will call me 'my husband'; you will no longer call me 'my master'" (vv. 15-16).

There's a little play on words going on here in the Hebraic language. The word for "master" that's used here is the same word as

"Baal."[1] God is saying essentially, "I am not an idol! I'm not just an idea! I'm not just a theology! I'm not just a philosophy! I'm not a means to an end!"

He is saying, "I Am that I Am. Would you love Me? Would you abandon everything else for this relationship?"

Don't lose simple devotion to Jesus. In whatever you do and however you approach it and whatever you're experimenting with, go for it. God's kingdom is wide. There's a narrow entrance, but once you step into this place, it's as wide and as free as anything you've ever experienced before. Just don't lose the simplicity of pure devotion.

Just don't lose the simplicity of pure devotion.

Now, I'm not sure if the desire of God's heart is to fix everything this side of heaven. It's really hard to follow God if you think that's what the mission is about. Whether you are in the arena of social justice or the arena of charismatic wackiness or the arena of allowing your theology to set your compass, it's all about Him. Could it really just be about Him?

MISSION AND RELATIONSHIP

In Acts 16:6, we get to read about an adventure—one of the apostle Paul's missionary journeys throughout the region of Phrygia and Galatia. But this passage says that the Holy Spirit kept Paul and those with him from preaching the Word.

Now again, the text isn't necessarily clear on how they knew that it was the Holy Spirit. I think it was a collaborative effort, because later, in verse 10, it says that they *concluded* that God called them to preach in Macedonia. They pooled their information. Someone had a vision, someone had a sense, and someone else just thought,

This isn't so smart. It was a combination of things.

The text does make it clear that there was some kind of collaborative discussion that happened among Paul and his companions, after which they concluded that they were supposed to go to Macedonia. But there was resistance. In verse 7, they had come to Mysia, and they were stopped. They tried to enter Bithynia, and they were stopped. The Holy Spirit didn't allow them to go into those places, so they had to adjust, reorient.

There was this definite initiation from God. They knew that the Holy Spirit had spoken to them. They knew they were supposed to carry the gospel message to other cultures. At the same time, they were partnering with God to discover their path. There's a level of interaction here that is really fascinating.

In Acts 16:8, they pass by Mysia and go down to Troas. It is important to note that Luke was the writer of Acts, as he was part of the team that traveled with Paul. We're reading Luke's memory of these events.

And what stuck out in Luke's memory was the awesome, open vision that Paul experienced. The truth is, Paul was the one who had the vision, but he didn't really talk about it.

But what did Paul remember most about why he went to Troas? Well, we know what was on Paul's heart from his own writings in 2 Corinthians 2:12-13. What did Paul remember? That he was looking for Titus! He wanted to see his buddy!

What had he learned about God? What had been modeled to him for the 20-plus years that he'd been a part of that emerging, growing community in Jerusalem?

Obviously, relationship was the key in that whole thing!

Remember, this was Paul, the guy who wrote a massive chunk of the New Testament. What motivated and pulled him? Apparently, one of the ways that God spoke intensely to Paul even trumped an open vision from God. God seemed to speak to Paul through his friendships and his relationships.

So in my understanding, relationship is really at the center of mission. Relationship with God, yes, but fascinatingly enough, relationship with each other as well.

I think God's also concerned about some of the interrelational dynamics we deal with every day. Maybe that's what Jesus was talking about in John 13:35 when He said, "People will know you follow Me by [by what?] your love"—what a novel evangelistic tool!

You see, if love's not at the center of our mission, people might be joining the Church, but I don't know if they're meeting God.

NOT TO THE LOST

In 2 Corinthians 2:15, we read that in the midst of the mission, we're to be an aroma. We create a fragrance. Out of our collision and interaction with the character and purpose of God, in the midst of the collision of the life of community, an aroma is created.

Who is this aroma for? This has just been blowing my mind.

Are we an aroma to the lost? The searching? The poor? The broken? Is that right? No, it's to God. What? The mission and the aroma of our mission are for God. "For we are to God the aroma of Christ among those who are being saved and those who are perishing" (2 Corinthians 2:15).

In some ways, the lost aren't even the mission at all. The purpose is worship. Here's the trick. If you understand worship, you understand that God can't even receive worship if it's not attached to loving our neighbors. You know Matthew 22:37,39: "'Love the Lord your God with all your heart and with all your soul and with all your mind.' And the second is like it: 'Love your neighbor as yourself.'"

Again, 2 Corinthians 2:15-16 says, "For we are to God the aroma

of Christ among those who are being saved and those who are perishing. To the one we are the smell of death; to the other, the fragrance of life."

Does this mean that even if we used the right PowerPoint presentation in church or showed the right movie clip, some people would still reject Jesus? It's kind of hard to get comfortable with that idea, but I think you've got to be comfortable with it or it will mess up your mission. You'll start trying to do something you can't do. You can't save anybody. You're to be the aroma of Christ to God.

Now look at what Paul says. Here he is, showing his vulnerability again: "And who is equal to such a task?" (2 Corinthians 2:16). I think that the inference of the text is this: Who's equal to this task? Nobody! This is the glory of the thing. Nobody can pull this off.

INTERGALACTIC CHRISTIANS

I want you to notice a few things about 2 Corinthians 2:17: "Unlike so many, we do not peddle the word of God for profit." Paul's saying that there are people, it would seem, who are uncomfortable with the collision that the gospel brings to culture.

I'm not talking about the collision with our idiotic religiosity. I'm not talking about the collision with our petty Christian ease. I'm not talking about the collision with the weird subculture, ghetto thing that we've created. I'm not talking about that, because I would assume that's not the reason why Paul was running into opposition. He's saying, "Man, who is equal to this task? There is so much pressure in this thing because we want it to work." I do love people. I do care. But if I'm really honest with myself, under the layer of love and care is this insecurity in me that propels me to also want to be successful, to sell the book on the back table. I want to be part of the cool, happening thing that's being taken notice of.

I was at a conference the other day where there were all these big-named speakers from across the spectrum of Christianity in attendance. I was sitting at the far end of the head table, and the microphone was going down the line, from person to person to person, as each shared his or her biography. I'm sure it was insecurity—I don't think they were trying to do this—but as the microphone went from one person to the next, the ministries seemed to get bigger and more impressive. They were becoming intergalactic. I mean, we were having aliens coming to Christ and alternative communities springing up on Venus.

There I was, sitting at the end of the table—it was the first time since I was 17 years old that I wasn't on a church staff or planting a church. I was sitting there, going, *Oh God, what am I going to say?* The mic came to me, and it felt like one of those bad teen movies. You know, where the guy comes up to the mic and everything gets incredibly quiet. I didn't really process what I was going to say; it just came out of my mouth.

"Well, trash day is Monday," I said. "In Los Angeles we have this black plastic bin with little wheels, and you put all the regular trash in there. And there's a green bin in which you put all the lawn cuttings and grass trimmings. Then there's this really big blue bin for the recyclables. You've got to roll them down to the curb and follow specific regulations. There has to be a certain amount of space between each one because those big trucks with mechanical arms come, so you can't have them too close together. I take the trash to the curb, and then I take my kids to school."

Then I just handed off the mic and the room was quiet—like deathly silent.

There's pressure. There's a lot of pressure.

The writing of 2 Corinthians 2 couldn't have been too far into the history of the Church, and what was already happening? There were people peddling the Word of God for profit.

There are so many weird things going on in the landscape of Christianity right now with regard to money and products and sales and charts.

It also has become sort of hip to try and blow up the existing systems and structures, but it seems like we've just created another system in the process. We've plugged ourselves in, and maybe it looks a little cooler or it utilizes technology more effectively. I'm just going, *God, am I losing myself in the middle of this somewhere?* The whole worship-industry explosion is just mind-boggling, in terms of the amount of money that's swirling around. You know, I'm not saying it's bad, but it creates pressure, especially in a consumer-driven culture, which is bigger than North America—it's becoming an international dynamic.

GOING OUT

In Matthew 10, Jesus sent out the apostles, the disciples, the sent ones, on their first strategic, missional adventure. Then He said the most bizarre thing to them: Leave your money at home; don't make this about money (see v. 9). The disciples were probably thinking, *But we could really do the mission well if we had a bigger budget. We could really do the mission if some rich dude would get saved and pour it in here. Forget his even being saved.*

Another thing Jesus says, more or less, is brace yourselves and just hang on. You are going to be sent out like sheep among wolves (see v. 16).

We hate that! We want to be the wolf pack. We want to stand shoulder to shoulder with the marketplace, with the entertainment industry. Please understand, I'm an artist to the very core of my being, and I love the excellence of what is happening in the Christian entertainment industries. But sometimes that excellence can suddenly get into the driver's seat. We think that if we could just be on the mountain with Elijah, just standing shoulder to shoulder with the prophets of ages past, boy could we ever show them!

It's like James and John saying to Jesus, "Call down fire, man! Let's do it! Let's burn them up, baby!" (see Luke 9:54). Let's take over the politics. Let's take over the entertainment industries. Let's take over the marketplace. We want to walk in the center of town and growl like a wolf and watch the pack come to us. We want everybody to take notice. But Jesus basically says, "You're going to walk into the middle of town and baaahh! like a sheep" (see v. 55). And we think that's just horrible. It's simply not as impressive.

Now, can we be impressive? Of course. But go to 2 Corinthians 4, which begins, "Since through God's mercy we have this ministry." Through God's mercy we have this mission—not through our ability, our talent or our presence.

"Through God's mercy . . . , we don't lose heart" (v. 1).

So for goodness' sake, I can't preach myself. I must preach Christ as Lord and refer to each other as "servants for Jesus' sake" (v. 5). "For God, who said, 'Let light shine out of darkness,' made his light shine in our hearts to give us the light of the knowledge of the glory of God in the face of Christ. But we have this treasure in jars of clay" (vv. 6-7).

I carry this in a broken vessel, in a weak vessel. It could just drop and shatter at any moment. But there's good news: God's glory still shines through that, and it would appear that that is actually where the glory of God dwells. That was another stunning thing about Jesus. The prophecies were that the glory of God would come to the Temple. What did it look like? Jesus.

The God who could have come in strength and might and power chose weakness. Weakness is not sin. What did the writer of Hebrews say? Jesus learned obedience through suffering (see 5:8). Well, what would Jesus have had to learn anyway? What did He learn? He had to expand; He had to grow. Taking this journey and embracing this path are not in contradiction with holiness or perfection or godliness. So many times we've put those things in opposition to each other, and I think it's damaged our abilities to be missional and to present the truth of the gospel.

COLLISION
Dialogue with David Ruis

Practitioner 1: My heart hurts when I read so-called emergent literature that says that the Church is the enemy, when the emergent culture is also part of the Church. We are all the people of God. But sometimes I feel like the traditional church has been deserted by the emergent church and is not invited to come along. But I also realize that the traditional church has said of the emergent church, "You guys are too noisy. Why don't you go do that over there?" I'm wondering about your thoughts on what bridges are most successful to invite the traditional church to come along with the emergent church, and also to allow the emergent church to learn from the traditional church?

The heart of unity through the template of Scripture is the ability to bless each other to be who we are.

David: I can only respond from my experience. I think we have to be careful that we don't minimize the intensity of longing for something real. We can't minimize the gift of tension that the collisions of these discussions will bring to the table.

I've heard the fear in the institutional side of Christianity, a fear that the emerging leaders are writing off the Church. I don't feel that, but I do feel a lot of passion. I feel a lot of angst. I feel a lot of longing. And so I don't really have an answer, but I think there needs to be space for dialogue.

To me, unity is not doing everything together in the same place, in the same way. I think that the heart of unity through the template of Scripture is the ability to bless each other to be who we are. So go and do what God's telling you to do. If it means you can't get to a crusade gathering down at the stadium on Saturday, that doesn't mean you're not into unity. It means that your schedules aren't lining up or there's a different approach you'd rather try—do you know what I'm trying to say?

Look at Matthew 9:16-17:

> No one sews a patch of unshrunk cloth on an old garment, for the patch will pull away from the garment, making the tear worse. Neither do men pour new wine into old wine skins. If they do, the skins will burst, the wine will run out and the wineskins will be ruined. No, they pour new wine into new wineskins, and both are preserved.

Let's look at the last phrase: "And both are preserved." I think it could mean something.

There's a tendency throughout Church history to try to mix things together that really aren't intended to be mixed together, and everybody loses. The wine spills out, and it's gone. The wineskin busts open, and it's like you can't put Humpty Dumpty back together again. There is often pain and sorrow and suffering just in the collision. Maybe a way forward is that under the grace of God and by the help of the Holy Spirit, we can learn how to preserve both.

Practitioner 1: For me, the difficulty is in the definition; help me with your definition of "church." If your definition is that it has a 501(c)(3) status, then I'm not sure that helps me understand what it is. If your definition is a one-hour event one day a week, I'm not sure that helps me understand "church" either. If your definition is that it has a paid staff and has a vision or a purpose statement or something, with a ministry plant, that doesn't help me understand it.

I am not against the Church. I'm just not sure that the church as a wineskin, especially in America, helps Christ's movement worldwide. And I think that what we've done is exported and processed the Church into a shrink-wrapped system. When I state, "Here's another way of looking at church," it's not an attack against them. But the Church today seems to hold the power and say, "If you don't do church the way I'm doing church, then you're not in church. You're not part of the Church." I would rather be in society where that's church and this is church. Most of the world would define "church" simply as a small group. And that truly is church for them. So I'm not antichurch; I just want to think about church beyond the traditional idea of it. Is that fair?

David: Does someone want to respond to that?

Practitioner 2: My definition of "church" is the capital *C* church. I pastor a traditional church that has an emerging-church culture trying to bubble out of it. And I'm wrestling with how to lead the traditional part of my church to a fresh new spirituality. But 70-year-olds don't see fresh new spirituality as a necessity. I'm not willing to write them off as dead, because I'm called to lead them to spiritual health. So in our church, we're inviting our traditional church members to experience an emerging-church spirituality with community groups and with life-transformation groups and that sort of thing. We're calling them to genuine relationship with each other and with the community again, but in a 130-year-old church, it's tough to lead that generation into this new experience of spirituality.

Practitioner 1: I personally believe that those who are aged 70 and above have a church that they love. You don't want to close the door on that. Do you know what I mean? I think that the emerging group has another church tailored for them. So my question is, How do these groups coexist without buying into either's product? One loves the organ. Give it to them. I mean, let's not pull it out. In the modern church, we said, "Everybody's got to do it the same way that we do it." So how can we honor, love and respect everyone's tradition and yet rally around one Spirit and one baptism?

David: Let me throw out just one thought at the end of that. Is there something underneath all the shrink-wrap that you're longing for? What is this? It might demand some crumbling of structure. You're longing to see your 70-year-olds deeply engaged spiritually. In some ways, that's almost the step that's before the organ or the electric guitar or the "Do we meet on Sundays?" question. Sometimes our arguments and attempts at packaging it better actually get in the way of those spiritual encounters. I know that's complex, but I'm just adding another dimension to this conversation.

Practitioner 3: I think the point is that on one level or another, and what some of us are just beginning to discover, the Church is *always* supposed to be "emergent."

Since Eden, we've all had a yearning put into us to find paradise, which is something that we'll eventually experience with the Lord when we step into that place that we can rightfully call home. But until that time, we live in this tension, the tension between what we truly long to do and the realization that the Lord has us moving and moving and moving. Living in that tension is the place that He's really called us to, because the Church emerges every day. The Spirit of God moves every day.

So I think the point is really two things: One, the Church's destiny is to always emerge and to become. And two, I'm stricken by how consumed we get with the wineskins, when God's concern is delivering the wine. If there's anything that we can learn about the wineskins, it is that the skins themselves aren't the point. The point is the wine that's inside. If our missional goal in life is to bring the fragrance of God's presence into the reality that we find ourselves in, then there always will be a tension and a back stock of both old and new wine, as there should be. They both have their purpose and their place. And they both can get muddled up if our focus is on building wineskins and not on delivering wine.

TO END

It's important to take this discussion into our own communities, into our own churches, into our own contexts. The goal isn't to get an answer or to draw a conclusion, but simply to invite the Holy Spirit into the conversation and to allow Him to speak to each of us. This discussion isn't about solving these questions necessarily. It is about interaction. I don't want to find the Church as much as I want to find Jesus. I think that if I find Him, then I'll find the Church.

NOTE

1. James Strong, *The New Strong's Exhaustive Concordance of the Bible* (Nashville, TN: Thomas Nelson Publishers, 1984), Hebrew ref. no. 1180.

chapter 6

JUSTICE COLLABORATIVE

Pete Greig, Doug Pagitt, David Ruis, Joyce Heron and Jackie Pearce

TO BE RADICAL
Monologue by Pete Greig

I'll assume you know that the word "radical" is overused, so much so that it's almost empty of meaning these days. But it actually means "from the root."[1] So to be truly radical is to go back to the roots of a thing. My concern for us in being radical is that we want to be people who are defined by the simplicity of living for Jesus Christ.

You may or may not be aware of the liberation theologians of South America who came up with the idea of praxis, which means that the only people who can read the Bible right are the people who actually act on its teachings. If you are just tucked away in some nice seminary somewhere or you're living in some kind of massive compromise, you may read the Bible right, but your theology will end up being a bit off so that you spiritualize Scripture. *Oh, this passage is just about the "spiritually poor" who are driving around in their BMWs*, you may think to yourself. We have to believe that a passage might actually, literally be about the poor.

If we want to see right, if we want to speak with authority and if we want to be truly missional, then there are three areas in our lives that we need to focus on. Everything else is secondary. The first is our private spirituality. There are people who speak a lot about what God is or isn't doing and where culture is at, but quite frankly they don't have a private spirituality. As such they will say impressive things, but it doesn't bear fruit. The second is this: I believe it's important for us to be kind to people. To me this means that we're engaged with those whom we, by nature of being a community, marginalize. The moment that we define ourselves as a group or a people, there are people outside the group, such as the poor, the oppressed and those who don't share our worldviews. We also will not find true revelation and true authority unless we're engaging with people who don't know Jesus. The whole deal of connecting with people who don't know Jesus and allowing them to shape our thinking is part of our having our theology right. The third thing, I believe, is that it's important to live in community. I meet lots of academic type people with Ph.D.s in the areas of postmodernity, but they're highly individualized. They're not really doing their thinking in community. As far as I'm concerned, we need to be living at the juxtaposition of those three things.

Now, I think it's very important that we allow each other to disagree here. We need to come to this discussion of justice issues with humility and the ability to say, "I may be wrong." And most of all, we need to come saying, "It's impossible for me to have a full picture of this on my own."

THE ECONOMICS OF BEING A GOOD NEIGHBOR
Monologue by Doug Pagitt

We're supposed to be exploring "the communal postures of justice and worship and prayer among the poor." I think this is a great sentence, because I like complicated sentences that could go a few different directions. The place in this sentence that I started to think about was the term "the poor." First of all, I think that defining "the poor" matters in this conversation. In North America, we talk about people here living in poverty, and I think that we use the word "poverty" in a way that doesn't do much value to the word itself. I'm not sure that people in the United States are truly in poverty, when it's looked at in comparison with the global situation of the poor.

In our Minneapolis community, I'm really caught up in the complexities of the difference between people who don't yet have the money that they need and those who are truly poor, meaning they could never get the money that they need. The Hispanic families that we work with are just poor for a while. They are not going to be poor forever. They have a strong work ethic, and they'll learn how to work the system. There are other people in our neighborhood, oftentimes poor white families or African-American families, stuck in more systemic problems, and there doesn't seem to be any solution. Now that's a different situation from what happens in Guatemala and Jamaica and other places.

So it gets really complicated when I see the term "the poor." It also complicates it for me because I know that most of our *theology of the poor* in North America evangelicalism comes out of work that the Christian Community Development Association (CCDA) has done. If you're not familiar with that group, it's been very active. Its central concept is to relocate, to redistribute and to reconcile. Those are its three major emphases about how you make a difference in the world.

It's my opinion that the CCDA was developed rightly and properly during a time when global economics was in a period of scarcity, meaning there wasn't enough. You could've said to someone, "Eat what's on your plate. There are people starving in China," and rightly so. It's also my opinion that we don't live in a world of economic scarcity anymore; we live in a world of surplus. Our problem is not that we have too little food or too few economic resources; the problem is the poor distribution system that's funneling food through complicated global mechanisms and multinational corporations. All of which is to say, we live in an industrialized, global economy that's no longer made up of simple agricultural societies. Christianity has played out the great majority of its history and a great majority of its theology in agrarian societies that don't exist in this world anymore.

We have to be engaged with the question, What does it mean to be a people who are involved in systems of poverty in our world that go beyond any personal involvement that we have?

When I see terms like "the poor," I begin to think that I don't know anything that goes on in the world, that I don't know enough about the poor. But I have these people living outside my door, and I have adopted foster children in our family, so I understand several levels of this. When Jesus says things about the poor, it challenges me to learn more about them, because I don't think that I even have the slightest inclination of what I have to know to be engaged with them.

I still struggle with the fact that I drive around in my car listening to NPR and I tend to know what's going on around the world more than I know what's going on in the street that I'm driving on.

The world has changed in some profound ways that make it a real issue for me to live as a good neighbor. So in my life, I've had to reduce all of this down to a question: How do I live as a good neighbor and never remain satisfied with that being enough? I'd love to have a conversation about what it means to truly live as a good neighbor in the world that we all live in—especially to those people who literally live right next door.

REMEMBER THE POOR
Monologue by David Ruis

It's fascinating to ask, "Jesus, how do I posture myself in the midst of all this poverty?" I have a friend named Jackie Pullinger who works in Hong Kong among really impoverished people, including a lot of heroine addicts and drug addicts and real people living on the fringes of Chinese society. She's been working there for 30-plus years. People always want to go work with her, and she needs help and lots of assistance, but I've heard her say so many times, "Go and find your own poor." Almost like, "Leave my poor alone. You discover who your poor are."

I've got this theory that if we do have eyes to see people, it has to be within our neighborhoods, even more than we realize. In the book of James, there is a fascinating template of community. It is my understanding that it was the first New Testament book written—chronologically it was written before the Gospels—and James wrote with this unbelievable passion about the Christian community's losing its moorings if it loses its connection with marginalized people. James writes, "Has not God chosen those who are poor . . . ?" (2:5). Later in the verse, he says that the poor are the chosen of the earth, which is a whole bizarre discussion in itself.

James qualifies his question immediately: "Has not God chosen those who are poor *in the eyes of the world*" (emphasis added). He's essentially saying, "Don't let your brain go somewhere that God doesn't want it to go. Don't worry about some of the other issues. Don't spiritualize this." There are circumstances in our societies and our cultures wherever we are, whether it's in North America or the backwoods of Nepal, in which we come face-to-face with what poverty looks like, what it smells like and what that stirs up in us.

I'm fascinated to wrestle with what it means to have poor people at the center of our community identity, whether it's actually tangible people sitting there in church. Whatever the case, the poor are colliding with us constantly, not as an outreach or a program, but as individuals who are part of the mix of the community. This is critical for me in understanding how God views true community, how we embrace the poor and what it does for me, more than what I do for them. What stereotypes stir up in me? What unconscious prejudices flush to the top when I encounter the poor in the eyes of the world?

The key question is, Are the poor central to the gospel or not?

When Jesus said He came to preach good news to the poor, who did He mean?

The last church-planting adventure my family and I went on was some years ago in a city just above Winnipeg in Canada. I remember sitting in my study, getting ready for this new adventure, with books and tapes and demographic studies; church growth this, megachurch that; and on and on.

I had my Bible lying on my desk, and I was looking at Galatians 2:10, which is where Peter, James and John sent Paul and Barnabas out to preach the gospel for the first time. The Church had been scattered. As they went, the believers were taking the gospel everywhere and spreading it around the world. But here we see the first strategic decision to send them out, and it's deliberate. Paul went before these three pillars of the Church, and they gave him one requirement.

I looked at all of the books on my shelf, all the teachings, all the tools, and I thought, *One requirement!? Nobody ever told me! I feel ripped off by all the money I spent on books and the theology degree—and all the effort. Nobody told me the one thing.* Of course, the one thing is "that we should continue to remember the poor." And Paul's response is just as shocking as that statement, as he says, "[It was] the very thing I was eager to do."

I remember sitting in northeast India; it was one of my first experiences in a Third World context. I was with about 150 people who were just trying to live life for Jesus in areas of the world that are persecuted, where Christianity is illegal. These people were from Bhutan or Tibet or the rural areas of Nepal.

There we were, 150 of us huddling in a little room for a meeting. I came from North America, where I had been wrestling with poverty in the inner city of Winnipeg, and now I saw a whole other level of poverty. I was completely undone. I was looking at the poorest people I had ever seen. These people, who didn't even eat three meals a day, were in rags, in tatters, and they were tangibly dirty, as they didn't have clean water.

One afternoon, we were just chatting and interacting through the translator and a thought started to bug me. I think it was God, trying to get my attention. This is the thought that was in my head during the conversation: *Tell them Galatians 2:10. Tell them Galatians 2:10?* I questioned. *Tell them Galatians 2:10.*

I thought to myself, *But these are the guys I'm not supposed to forget.* Like, how much gall would it take to look someone, in their situation, in the face and say, "Don't forget the poor"? It didn't make sense to me in the slightest but I could not escape the thought: *Tell them not to forget the poor. Tell them.*

So I started to explain Galatians 2:10. A good friend of mine says that you should make a short story long, so I just started to unpack the passage for these people. I didn't really have a chance to explain all of it, but even still, people's guards started dropping. People were reacting physically. I felt like I had crossed the proverbial cultural mistake line or something. So I asked my translator, "What's happening?"

He replied, "They're repenting."

I said, "What? Like, what?"

Then the stories start coming out about how these men had encountered blessing and how many of them carried some measure of leadership in their churches and communities. They were becoming men of God.

But these men had begun to distance themselves and to feel better than some of the others. Now, I would look at their context and think, *That is poor like from top to bottom, but within their poverty are layers of poverty.*

GOD'S BIAS TOWARD THE POOR
Monologue by Joyce Heron

How do we approach mercy ministry (or should that be referred to as Christian tourism in poor neighborhoods)? I've spent my life in the downtown east side of Vancouver, Canada, which is one of the poorest neighborhoods in the city. Many people live in old hotels that are no longer hotels, buildings with basically 10 foot by 10 foot rooms and one bathroom a floor to share. The government provides this housing. Basically, in my neighborhood, I spend my life with people who are addicted to heroine and crack cocaine, and of those whom I have friendships with, many of them are mentally ill.

Out of the 5,000 needle users, 38 percent are AIDS positive. Out of that same group of people, 67 percent are HIV positive. And out of that same group of people, 92 percent of them are hepatitis-C positive. In my neighborhood, everyone is dying. I'm not trying to be dramatic. I'm just telling you the truth. That's the reality that I live with and work in every day.

People I work with say to me, "You're smart and articulate, and you could be making lots of money. Why do you live here and do this with us?" I can speak only about what I see in the Scripture. Did you know that if you cut holes in your Bible in all the places that it talks about the importance of the poor, that you would be astounded by how many places you would be able to see through it? Scripture references the poor and oppressed ("needy," "orphans," "widows" and so on) over 400 times.

I have come to the conclusion that God has an absolutely massive bias toward the poor, and that as one of His followers, I'm supposed to manifest the same bias. Let me illustrate this bias with an anecdote: If I had kids, and one of them was being picked on at school all the time, my concern for that particular child would be increased in comparison with my concern for the other children. In the same way, I think that God is increasingly concerned for the poor and for those who are oppressed and marginalized.

I've come to the conclusion that God has an absolutely massive bias toward the poor, and that as one of His followers, I'm supposed to manifest the same bias.

I think we need to wrestle with that and figure out whether we believe this for ourselves. And whatever we do, we have to do more than just set up programs. What we have to do is actually become friends with people who are marginalized. And if we start there, chances are, it's going to change us.

Now, it's hard for an evangelical type of mind to believe that you could actually meet God in a heroine addict or that a crack addict could actually know Jesus. Some of them don't know God, but they all bear His image, because all of us are made in His image (see Genesis 1:27). We can always bump into God in another. So I guess that some of the big questions I'm asking are these: Can justice be relegated to a department of a church, or should it be a function of every believer? If it should be a function of every believer, how does that get lived out? And if it's not being lived out, why not?

I'll give you an example. In my neighborhood, we have 84 nonprofit organizations. One third of them are faith based. So we have a Christian mission or program on every block. And they've been there for over 100 years, since the beginning of addiction in my neighborhood. The *Vancouver Courier* reported last year that every single day of the week we have over 100 evangelicals on our streets, passing out tuna sandwiches, hot chocolate and tracts, trying to lead people in the sinner's prayer. And it's not changing things.

I'm not saying that any of the programs are useless, but I just think there's something missing. And the thing missing is the fact that no one wants to be friends with these people. It's an "us and them" dynamic. It's downward relating. Do I think you need to set up a bunch of programs to feed the refugees and the poor in your neighborhood or take care of the single moms with three jobs or the working poor in your neighborhood or start a kids' club for the little kids without dads? I don't know.

My suggestion is, Absolutely not. If anything, become friends with some refugees, or with a single mom—and then you'll see that she's harassed. On Friday night, take her children, care for them and send her to get a haircut. Or befriend a man who's addicted to heroine or crack cocaine and invite him over to your house for a barbecue, but maybe you're not sure what he is going to do and how rude he might be.

There is one thing we all need more than anything else, and nothing ever changes us except this thing: loving human relationships. If a loving human relationship is the thing that's changed me or the thing that's changed you, the same is true for the poor.

My five-year-old nephew rebuked me one day as he was going through my wallet, asking about money. I said that it was for God and told him what God needs my money for. At one point, I said, "And some of it goes to the poor. Some of it goes to other countries, and it helps people to know about Jesus."

He interrupted me, "No, Auntie, no! Not 'the poor,' but 'the poor *people*,' Auntie, 'people'!"

I thought, *There it is. Out of the mouth of babes.* These people aren't something to label or categorize. They're actually people. But we don't see them as people until they're our friends. I am absolutely horrified and angry that people use objectifying language like "pimps," "prostitutes," "the homeless" and "drug addicts." Do I identify all of my friends by the sexual abuses they've survived? By their problems? By their vocation or the fact that they're divorced? No, I don't identify my friends by their problems. Our mentality about "the poor" only changes when we begin to relate to them as people.

THE INTENTION OF HUMANITY
Monologue by Doug Pagitt

I got into Christianity when I was 17, and over the next 13 years, this conversation about justice didn't come up much, other than sort of in a ubiquitous kind of way—like I'm probably supposed to be caring for the poor, but I probably shouldn't eat junk food either. Do you know what I mean?

It was almost as if caring for the poor really didn't matter, because the most important thing was the personal, intimate relationship that I had with God. For most people, that relationship with God is a private relationship, even though "personal" and "private" don't mean the same thing. It can be incredibly personal without being individualistic and private.

Well, I had what I call a second conversion of religious faith. I began to have suspicions that the Year of Jubilee (in the book of Leviticus), the Day of the Lord (in the book of Isaiah) and the kingdom of God (the expression that Jesus used) are all connected. The Jewish people had these practices that they were supposed to do, and the idea behind the practices was that everything counts, because everything in life matters to God. So the place of God is in the life that we live, not in an esoteric sort of individualized relationship with God.

I guess I didn't know how you were supposed to deal with the poor; I didn't have any concept. What did caring for the poor have to do with religion? I reasoned, *Well, good religious people are nicer than nonreligious people, and it's nice to take care of poor people.* That's about as far as I could get with it.

Caring for the poor is not just some "Christian" agenda item. It's not like Jesus came with an agenda to be nice to the poor, and if we're Christians, we have to have His agenda. *This truth is that caring for the poor is the intention of humanity.* And we can't fully live as human beings if we continue to exploit and to marginalize those whom we're supposed to care for.

This issue is not about how I can be more "Christian"; it is about how I can be more human. And I happen to think that the pursuit of humanity is the pursuit of Christianity. For me, this paradigm shift took caring for the poor out of the religious category. I was commissioned to care for them the moment I shot out of my mother's womb, not the moment I decided that I wanted to be more serious about Jesus.

Sometimes Christians sort of look down on the Law, but if you look at the Old Testament, you'll find whole systems of caring for the poor. The Jewish people canceled debts in the fiftieth year, the Year of Jubilee, and did all sorts of other things. So when Jesus talked about forgiving our debts as we forgive our debtors, He wasn't making up a new ethic; He was harkening back to the year of the Jubilee.

THE INTENTION OF HUMANITY
Dialogue with Joyce Heron

Joyce: We need to ask the Lord to give us eyes to see. The point to the story of the Good Samaritan is twofold. First, the Samaritan was a marginalized person himself. Second, the Samaritan saw the man and acted. But we have to start by asking God to give us eyes to see. And then when we see, we have to do something. Now, our hearts get hardened because we have watched World Vision on TV and have seen poor people and children with bloated bellies. I say, just offer God a week, hoping that you'll see one person over that time period. You might be surprised what God does. I'm not saying that I have all the answers, but . . .

Practitioner 1: That makes sense.

Practitioner 2: I would say that even if you feel like you're being fake, just keep trying. What harm can come out of it, really? If you're trying to do something good, just keep trying and eventually you'll get it. You didn't start off knowing all the answers. You started off and you were "fake." You start learning as you go along.

Joyce: Well, it isn't even falseness, really. It's an uncomfortable tension.

Practitioner 2: I guess it's just awkward and unnatural.

Joyce: So you're not lying about your posture; you're just uncomfortable with it. I think the other thing is that I don't think everyone should do what I do. If hundreds and thousands of Christians and evangelicals moved to the streets, we would displace all the poor, and then they would have nowhere to go. That would be really stupid, right? The point is that you have to have a radical transformation in your life and in your perceptions.

Practitioner 3: It's a complicated and big world, and all of us who have been around the world and lived in other places want to get up and go live somewhere else with some of these people. This action goes well beyond helping to change their situation of never owning any property to actually owning something. It's bigger than that. We don't have the capability to deal with mental illness; we don't have the capability to deal with addictions; and we don't have the capability to deal with all the sexual abuses from predators. We continue to do it over and over; and every time it fails, we just say, "That's not the point." It is not like we are the wealthy ones who aren't poor anymore. Remember how after September 11, people around the world prayed for the people in America because of the terrorist attacks? Well, there's this reciprocity that takes place.

Joyce: I have so many friends who are dying, and we get teams of people together to wait with them around the clock until they die, so they know that they won't die alone. We just sit with them, pray with them, worship with them, read Scripture aloud and journey with them into death.

At the end of the day, I don't think it's the missional mandate of the Church to fix heroine addiction or mental health. We're called to love, though a person's problem might never change.

I'll tell you about my friend Joe. He's 58 years old and he's a native, First Nations, Indian. When Joe was three years old, his parents were killed in an accident; he was in his house on the reserve, but no one knew. For almost two weeks he was by himself. When Joe finally was found, he was almost dead.

Joe then was put in the foster system. When he had been in the system for only a few months, the social worker found out that he was being abused, so he was moved into another house. But there a foster parent kept putting cigarettes on his body, so again he was moved to another house. By the time he was five, he had "anger issues"—no kidding. And then he became the problem, so he got bumped and bumped and bumped.

When he was 11—I know this is grotesque, but it is the truth about my friend's life—his foster parents sold him to a man who sexually abused him for three years. This makes you wonder, *How can that happen? How can the government lose a child?* Well, it happened. Joe escaped from that situation when he was 14, and he's been addicted to heroine ever since.

I'll tell you what: Joe needs Jesus. He did a year of Bible college at some point and cleaned up for a while. I don't know exactly what happened to him, but someone said something awful to him and he left.

So I sat down with him and said, "Joseph, we all have the same starting out place in life, in our humanity. Someone might look at me and say, 'Wow, she's a superturbo Christian because of the things she does' or 'because of x, y or z'; and they can see that I've walked this far. But in God's economy, Joseph, you may have walked double the distance, because of all the stuff you've had to walk through. So your maturity actually may be greater than mine or anyone else's." You know, this is a very upside-down way to look at things. I can learn from Joseph. It's not about his becoming like me.

I think you have to ask yourself some very important questions about your life. Why have you participated in marginalization? Behind each of these stories you may find—not all the time, but most of the time—years of oppression and abuse and horror that you don't even understand. And I think there's a massive difference between mercy and justice.

BOUNDARIES
Monologue by Jackie Pearce

My name's Jackie Pearce, and as a parent, I'd like to add something. There are two things that we do in our homeless ministry, and we do them *just* to establish relationship, which is obviously really important in forming friendships. Once you've formed a friendship, there is a learning process that takes place within yourself. I have learned so much from the people that I've encountered, especially because I also live in a downtown area with my family, which brings a really important subject into this. I have two small children who have a lot of needs, and I have a husband who has needs too.

I've been engaging in the lives of others and bringing my kids alongside, and I think it is very important for them to see another side of life, to see people with needs. It's been really rewarding to see my son, who is three years old, talking to a woman whom a lot of people in the community disdain. She is a woman who is not easy to get along with, and we've willingly been helping her in different things—but I want to emphasize, within limits. I could get a phone call from her at any hour of the day. I could be calling for resources on her behalf every day. She's deaf and she's in a wheelchair. There are a lot of issues going on in her life. But one Sunday my son said, "Where is Melanie? I love her." That's been really rewarding to see.

At the same time, I have learned that I have to set limits—I have to set boundaries—and I have to balance meeting her needs with meeting those of my family. My family comes first, next to my relationship with Christ. I've had to stress that to a lot of the people I've encountered while working with those who live on the streets, the really poor people. I feel like this needs to be addressed too, as a balance, because I think that God has limits and boundaries for all of us to live by—poor people have to live by them as well.

FRIENDSHIP
Monologue by David Ruis

Here are a few of my cascading thoughts: We can't underestimate the power of friendship. There's this puzzling idea in John 15:13, where Jesus says, "Greater love has no one than this, that he lay down his life for his friends." This makes no sense to me at all. It doesn't sound very impressive. How can laying down your life for your friends be the greatest love in the universe? I mean, isn't it more impressive to lay down your life for your enemy?

The fascinating part of this journey is that the more you move into the realm of friendship, life really does become about love. It's not about sacrifice, it's not about programs, and it's not about the strong helping the weak or the wealthy helping the impoverished. Friendship really changes the whole dynamic, and the next thing you know, you're pouring out your life in ways that are costly. But somehow it's not about the cost anymore—somehow you've transcended that—and you can touch it at any moment.

I had experienced this once while I was living in Winnipeg. There was a guy who was becoming part of our community, and for some reason he was the one guy I had the most trouble with—we clashed in every way. Everyone called him One Wing Wayne, because he passed out once near the railroad track, his arm dangling on the track, and a train came and just took his arm clean off.

So he's got this prosthetic arm with a hook. He used to drive us nuts with his hook, because he'd hook us and pinch us all the time—and it hurt! He was an obnoxious kid; but he was the greatest gift to me, because I had to serve him and deal with so much junk because of my relationship with him.

One day, I was on my way to our ministry center, where we would gather together as a community. I was walking a couple of blocks through the north end of town, the sort of place you're not supposed to go. I was about to cross the street when out of the corner of my eye, I saw Wayne coming down another street. I thought to myself, *Oh man, what am I going to do? Do I have time to talk to him?*

There was a crack house on that street corner, and a couple of gang guys came out onto their front stoop area and started to yell at him, "Hey, sniffer!" In that cultural context, up in central Canada, the sniffers are below the bottom rung. They won't even admit that they do it. They'll admit to heroine, crack, alcohol, anything; but they won't admit to sniffing the rag, because doing that puts you off the bottom rung. At first, Wayne was coming along, sort of aloof and stumbling a little, but then he started to freak out and chatter nervously.

So the crack house was on the corner, Wayne was walking up to it, and I was walking right into the middle of this thing, thinking, *I think I read about this once. The problem is, I know the answer to the story. I know what greater love is supposed to look like. Am I really going to be able to, like, pull this off?* Wayne was fast becoming my neighbor, and I was on my way to church, but I was thinking that this was a test I wasn't sure I wanted to pass.

The guys got more and more hostile. And Wayne didn't know what to do. He wasn't going to run, because they'd just go after him and take him down. So I was walking into this thing, and my heart was beating. I mean, it was scary. I don't want to overdramatize, but this doesn't happen every day.

Then before I could think about it—God must have been helping me, because I don't think I would have done this otherwise—I found myself yelling back, "Hey!"

The next thing I knew, the gang guys were turning, Wayne was turning, and everything started moving in slow motion. I thought, *Oh no. This is the big one hitting the fan.*

It was surreal. One of the gang guys actually yelled back at me, "What do you have to do with him?" That was his exact language. I'll never forget it. Then I felt something in that moment—I mean, I really felt it—and these words just came out of my mouth: "He's my friend!"

I felt something in that moment, and these words just came out of my mouth: "He's my friend!"

Half an hour later, this may not have been so true, but at that moment I felt like, *I think I can die for this guy*. Could it haven been supernatural? Maybe. I stepped into something relational that I had not tasted on behalf of someone like that before, and at that moment it wasn't about the programs, it wasn't about the right thing to do. In that moment it was about friendship.

Then reality kicked in. As I looked up, Wayne was tearing off, running down the street and around the corner as fast as he can go; and I was left facing these guys. There was an awkward moment between us, but thankfully, those words silenced them. I won't guarantee that that's the way to get out of an encounter with gang members, but it worked that day.

I think that God was teaching me about the very intriguing statement of Christ in Matthew 25:40: "Whatever you did for one of the least of these." I'm stunned at how many leaders are living among the poor in North America and around the world. That seems to be an identifying mark, if not *the* identifying mark, of how Christ recognizes us at the end of time.

STOP READING THIS

www.oxfam.com

ADBUSTERS.org

MAKE TRADE FAIR

Islamic Relief
Worldwide

www.islamic-relief.com

oneorphan.org

Christian Aid.co.uk

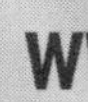

OOK

O BECOME CHANGE
IN OUR WORLD.

KEPOVERTYHISTORY.ORG

PROTEST 4

...a more just world www.protest4.co

...an end to human traffickin

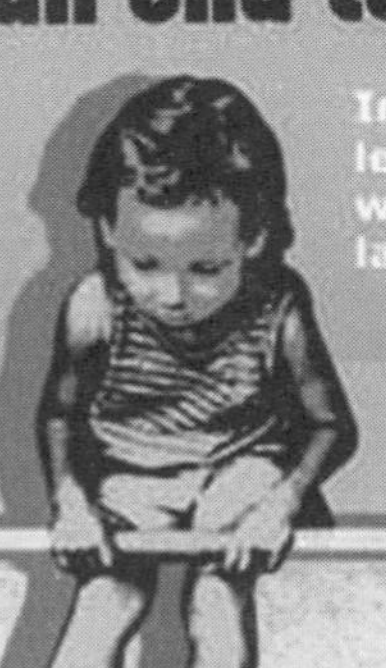

Incredibly in this day and age, at least 20 Million people around the world are trapped in bonded labour...

World Vision

worldvision.com

STOP READING AND GET INVOLVE
IN YOUR COMMUNITY, CITY, LOCA
NONPROFIT. FOR MORE IDEAS, GO
TO PRACTITIONERSBOOK.COM

A COMPLEX WORLD
Monologue by Doug Pagitt

I saw two documentaries recently. One was called *Bonhoeffer*. It was about Dietrich Bonhoeffer, a theologian in Germany, and how he and his family became part of a plot to assassinate Hitler. They brought a bomb into a meeting, but the bomb was positioned under the table in such a way that when it went off, the table blocked the shrapnel and Hitler didn't die. Dietrich Bonhoeffer was found to be an accomplice in the plot, so he was put in prison and was executed for it.

The other documentary I saw was called *Secretary*. It is the life story of Adolf Hitler's personal secretary, who, when she was interviewed just before she died, told what it was like working for Hitler. Fascinating.

The way she tells the story, Adolph Hitler was about to surrender when the Bonhoeffer assassination attempt occurred. When Hitler didn't die in the bombing, he was more convinced than ever that he was on a divine path ordained by God, because God had protected and saved him. It is unnerving to see the two sides of the Bonhoeffer story.

Bonhoeffer basically said that it was not just his job to pull victims out of the way; it was his job to stop a madman from driving down the road. But the very assassination attempt to stop the madman from driving down the road caused the end of the war to become even more brutal because, as a result, Hitler knew "for sure" that God was going to save him from destruction.

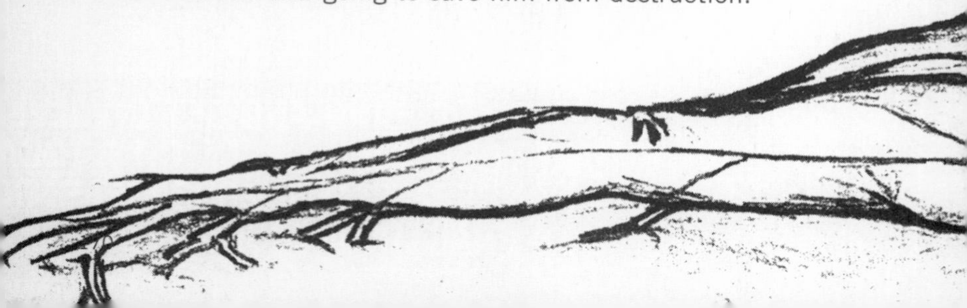

We live in an extremely complex world, don't we?

I come from the side of being a vigilante. I would just as soon go out and wreak havoc. Yet we must ask the question, How do we engage in stopping poverty without making it worse? We are engaged in a crazy world. We can go into a city or a country and bring about the help that we think we're going to bring, when 50 years later someone tells a story about how our "help" increased poverty all the more.

I don't think this takes the question off the table. I think it means that we must instead ask, Okay, so how do we step in and get involved in the world to make it better? If you move into a poorer neighborhood to be near the poor, you will displace a poor person. So you pay $650 a month to live in this place while you could afford $950 somewhere else, and now this poorer person doesn't have anywhere to live. You're there to help, but you're also causing more problems. This becomes a complex issue on every level. I don't know why Jesus didn't choose to get into these details. Maybe it was a different kind of world then. I don't know.

Do you think that maybe this causes us to rethink the kingdom of God? In our society, we are told to look this way, talk this talk and have this identity; but every time we buy into that philosophy, we communicate to the poor that their value is not going to be found until they match up to the message of this consumer society. Imagine a church, imagine the Body of Christ—all of us—somehow having formed our identity in Christ in such a way that we no longer communicate this message to the poor. Can it be done?

CAN IT BE DONE?

Go to www.practitionersbook.com and add your thoughts, insight, reactions, ideas, hopes and ways you are flushing this out in the context of your city.

NOTE

1. *Merriam-Webster's Collegiate Dictionary*, 11th ed., s.v. "radical."

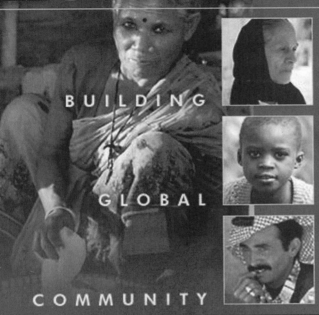

explorations of the

FUTURE OF THE CHURCH

Doug Pagitt

chapter seven

To generate this conversation, I asked some practitioners to help me. Here's what I did: I handed out a list of topics that I'd been thinking about (see figure 1) and asked the practitioners to choose items from the list that were interesting to them. Then I shared my thoughts on those items.

The hardest thing to do in that kind of setting is to take all the stuff that goes on in my life—the worries I have about friends in Jamaica who just moved there and are about to get hit by a hurricane; or about a person in our community who went through a gender transition surgery and who now thinks she wants to go back to being male; or about my son's game tomorrow morning and not knowing if I can get there by 6:00 a.m. and engage as a dad, after flying all night (without sleep) to get home—and to decide which of those things I want to share with you, hoping it connects.

I couldn't solve the fact that I had a zillion things going on in my mind, but I tried to solve the problem of my trying to determine, all on my own, what the conversation was going to be about.

FIGURE 1

1. I imagine a Church

1.1 that assumes God and not the Church to be the answer.

1.2 that joins in the work of God wherever it is found.

1.2.1 Our competition is not those who are seeking the good things of God, but rather those who are seeking to destroy the work of God.

1.3 where multiple voices are heard.

1.4 that is enthralled by the whole story of God.

1.5 with a deep ecclesiology.

1.6 with a "generous orthodoxy."

1.7 that is missional and seeks to live the agenda of God, not one based on our own vision.

1.8 that captures new wonderings and is not interested in being a hip version of a previous expression.

1.9 with a better understanding of the intentions of God.

1.10 that is a theological community doing theological work.

1.11 with optimistic, creative and greater imagination—the greatest fear is the loss of imagination.

1.12 with a different relationship with life ("If my life is for rent," Dido).

1.13 that steps into progressional preaching.

1.14 where there are spiritual formation communities, not religious service providers.

1.15 that has a higher view of the Bible than inerrancy allows.

1.16 that understands the kingdom of God as a holistic call.

1.17 that stops calling discipleship of Catholics evangelism.

1.18 that moves beyond the Reformation.

1.19 that uses spiritual formation beyond the educational model.

1.20 with historical, global, local and futuristic connections.

1.21 where the gospel is about everything—because everything matters.

1.22 that moves beyond Niebuhr's categories—there is no culture other than us; we are "they."

1.23 that sees itself in rhythmic harmony with God, not separate from God.

1.24 where community is the hermeneutic and the apologetic of the gospel.

1.25 where evangelism looks like all the options in Acts—especially like Peter's and Cornelius's.

1.26 where method and message both are progressing.

1.27 that is called to "enter" more than to "return."

2. I imagine leaders who

2.1 are educated in more arenas than just "religion."

2.1.1 I am troubled by seminary education, not because I think leaders do not need to be educated, but because seminaries provide too limited an education.

2.2 utilize different skills—listening, extracting, converging, poetics.

2.3 have an optimistic, progressive view of history.

2.4 are conversationalists in many arenas.

2.5 possess more feminine leadership qualities.

2.6 engage Scripture as "living and active."

2.7 understand church growth in terms beyond the comodification of Christianity.

2.8 become skilled in the contextual gospel.

2.9 have more metaphors for leadership.

2.10 live vulnerable lives.

2.11 learn from "their people" and all people.

3. I imagine a people who

3.1 live with open-eyed optimism.

3.2 are wholly developed.

3.3 see themselves as God's co-conspirators/co-collaborators.

3.4 live as useful religious people for the benefit of the world—moving beyond viewing Christianity as a "relationship with God."

3.5 take the call of the gospel to live beyond the American dream.

3.6 listen to the outsider with the same dignity and anticipation as the insider.

3.7 seek to "stop binary, reductionistic thinking now!"

3.8 live like life in the Body matters.

3.9 are about the kingdom of God and not a far away heaven.

3.10 do not see their lives as a distraction from God.

SEVERAL ASSUMPTIONS

Let me start with a few assumptions about what's happening in the world.

The first assumption I carry into this discussion is that we live in the greatest time in all of human history. Now, I recognize that this is not everyone's view of the world. I know that there are people who feel that we're in a digressive stage of human development, but I don't think so. I think that the only thing better than today is tomorrow. I think that this is a spectacular time in which to live. I don't think it's perfect, but I think it's better than every other time prior to this. I don't want to go back to the thirteenth century, the fifteenth century or the twentieth century. I think *now* is truly wonderful. So, some of my wide-eyed optimism comes out of that.

I also think that explorative creativity and imagination are essential to the human condition. I have this sense that part of the problem in our lives as we try to live in the twenty-first century is that there is a lack of imagination—sometimes progress stifles imagination, and sometimes progress fuels it. I think there's a real issue in terms of our imaginative lives.

I also believe that we live in a time of consistent, variable change. There has been no point of time in all of history when someone couldn't have said, "We live during a time of radical change." So I'm not going to suggest to you that we now live in a time of real change and that this is what's perpetuating some new thinking about God, some new thinking about church and some reimagining about how we're going to live in the world. We always do change, we always have been doing it, and we always will be doing it. We live in constant change, but the speed of that change is variable. There might be more changes at some periods of time and less at others. I would contend that the last 100 years have brought about a remarkable speed of change. That we as human beings live in situations that human beings previous to the last 100 years didn't live in. And that this has changed our understanding of ourselves, of God, of time, of humanity—of the whole thing.

My final thought on that point is that none of this change is a surprise to God. God is not surprised, and none of it is a problem for God. God is not bothered by human progress. In fact, I'm going to suggest that God is all about change.

Here's another assumption about the world: I think that the goal of the Church is to bring about a Year-of-Jubilee kind of love and care in the world. I think that we can see what the intention of God is for humanity, beyond just personal, individual salvation that leads us to another place after death. I think that God has an agenda for the world in which we live.

I think that this world is meant to be optimistic and forward leaning. God has called His people to "enter into the land," or enter into the world, which is something much greater than *returning* to the land from which we came. I don't think we're an exiled people, biding our time until we can return home. I think we're an Abrahamic people, being sent into the world.

We're not an exiled people, biding our time until we can return home. We're an Abrahamic people, being sent into the world.

I think that the goal of the world, and my hope for the world, is that we have an agenda of God that is open to all to participate in at varying levels of their understanding of the Christian story—that is, that people understand the Christian story as participants in the story; they don't have to understand it in order to participate in it.

Now that you know my assumptions, let's take a look at some topics that other practitioners found interesting.

I IMAGINE A CHURCH THAT IS MISSIONAL AND SEEKS TO LIVE THE AGENDA OF GOD, NOT ONE BASED ON OUR OWN VISION.

Practitioner 1: Can you talk about 1.7?

Doug: I imagine a Church that is missional and seeks to live the agenda of God, not one based on our own vision. Why did you choose this one in particular?

Practitioner 1: Well, because I'm a pastor who's responsible to create a vision—my congregation and board really want me to put on paper where it is we're going and why. My associate and I were sitting here and making notes that we just need to invite people to come and participate in a movement with God.

Doug: Personally I can connect with that thought on a couple of levels. This whole notion of being compensated financially for our role in our communities is really troublesome. In fact, I think there will be serious consequences for us if we don't answer the question, How in a twenty-first-century economy can we still pay people to be pastors?

Sometimes people erroneously talk a lot about "missionality," when what they're really talking about is a mission statement. That's not how I use the term. I would like to see a Church that says, "Look, whatever the agenda of God is in the world, we're going to enter into that agenda. And we don't know totally what that is."

Our role is not to outline a clear mission or vision statement to which we call people. Have you been trained to do that?

Practitioner 1: Yes.

Doug: I was trained to do that too, and we still kind of do that. We have people who have jobs in our church, who are on our staff, and we have just recently started saying to them, "Maybe we should write down your job description, because it's a little unclear whether you're doing anything at all." So we're coming up with job descriptions, but those aren't the same things as vision statements.

I can work up a vision statement. I can even pull out Proverbs 29:18, which says, "Where there is no vision, the people perish" (*KJV*). And we can paint a picture of a preferable future and then call people to it. So, being missional might really mean that we're supposed to say to one another, "What is our 'such a time as this'?" (to borrow a phrase from the book of Esther). When Esther was made queen, she didn't know why she was made queen, and Mordecai went to her saying, "Esther, there's going to be a slaughtering of all of our people, and maybe you've been made queen for such a time as this" (see Esther 4:12-14).

In other words, there is a reason why we are who we are. So the members of each community of faith need to discuss among themselves, *Who are we? What are we? Why are we here?*

Now, when I say that I'm imagining a Church, let me clarify that my community is not there yet on any of this stuff. We're trying to be there. At our church, we took on an attitude that was really driven by the two children that my wife and I adopted. When we adopted our kids, Ruben and Chico, we didn't say to them, "Okay, Ruben and Chico, we're the Pagitts. We have a way we're doing life already; and what we're going to try to do with you, as new members of our family, is to try to find ways for you to plug into it. We have an assimilation plan for you." We didn't say that. What we said to them was "This is who we are. Now you're joining us, and we're becoming not a bigger family but a new family."

Maybe our job as pastors, which might be worth paying someone to do, is to support the hopes and dreams of others, because the call of God to be missional people lies in the lives of these people. So we say to them, "Who are we? Why are we here?"

My church has met together for five years; and in the last couple of years, after some foundational thinking had already been done, other people have come and joined us. So we're beginning to relaunch this discussion in a conversational way, in which we say, "Look, we're not 12 people or 20 people anymore; now we're multiple hundreds of people. The same thing applies. We're to be new people with new understandings about what God has for us."

The problem with a vision statement is that it takes a long time to fulfill it, and you have to become a different kind of people in the very process of fulfilling it. The people you become at the end of fulfilling the vision does not represent the call that you once had in your lives.

We need to say to one another all the time, "Who are we now? What is God doing now? And what are we really supposed to do?" I think that if the job of the pastor or the leadership team or the core group or any of these exclusive groupings is to be the voice that tells the rest of the people the vision that God has for us, the church is not being a *missional community*.

I think that the question "What is the agenda of God and how are we uniquely postured to join into it?" should be a constant question that we ask each other, and I think that it's a question of implication over application. When we read the story of God, our job is to tell one another that we're *implicated* in the story of God, not that we're supposed to *apply* the story of God to ourselves. It seems that the call of God ought to implicate us so that we don't have the luxury of saying, "Well, I wonder what that has to do with me." Instead, we should be saying, "What do I have to do with God?"

I think it's a different sort of orientation, a different sort of call. Look, this is hard to get to. All of our structures and all of our music and all of our readings of Scripture and all of our support systems seem to be pulling in another way.

I IMAGINE LEADERS WHO POSSESS MORE FEMININE LEADERSHIP QUALITIES.

Practitioner 2: How about 2.5?

Doug: I can imagine leaders who possess more feminine qualities of leadership. I don't mean more effeminate. I mean creative, nurturing, drawing out. One of the problems I see is that in order for a woman to be a successful female leader in this world—to be rewarded and listened to and to achieve the kind of leadership role that she deserves—she has to act more masculine.

We have masculinized all leadership positions so that they're perceived as positions of power, not as positions of nurture. Look, there couldn't be anything more contrary to my personality. I am oriented totally toward leadership through big words, big dreams, big visions and other alpha-male sort of stuff. That's why I know what a failure that this kind of leadership produces in a community. We have to become stronger nurturing leaders.

I have a friend who says that the problem with the Church is the femininity of the Church. I'm like, "Dude, you couldn't be more wrong." There is this understanding of God that goes so far beyond male or female; our leadership needs to reflect His nature by living a nurturing, caring kind of life. I don't know who's going to lead us into that; it won't be a knucklehead like me. We have to find ways to be led by a multiplicity of voices, not by those of us who can simply draw the most attention.

There must be some way to become people who are more feminine, not effeminate, in our leadership.

Now I'm going to make a big reductionistic sort of statement. There was a period of time in the Early Church when leaders said that women couldn't lead—because in their culture, that would have caused a lack of growth of the community of faith. I wonder whether now we're in the position that men shouldn't lead for a while. Maybe men shouldn't lead until they (and I) get this worked out—because our cultural situation is such that it's destroying and choking out some things that it shouldn't. But that's probably just a binary reductionistic statement like, "Camping mocks the homeless." So I will mock myself in the middle of it.

I IMAGINE A CHURCH THAT STEPS INTO PROGRESSIONAL PREACHING.

Practitioner 3: Can you talk about 1.13?

Doug: 1.13? Okay, I'm trying to make up a word here, because I think we have an issue with preaching, in which we all acknowledge that it doesn't work. Everybody who does it acknowledges that it doesn't work. And we find different reasons why it doesn't work.

Some people say that today's preaching doesn't work because of the people. The people have changed, so our style of preaching doesn't fit them anymore. They like fast action and lots of visual cues, but we've got this linear style. So maybe we say the problem is that they think differently from what we can preach. Or the problem

REFLEC

reminder

is that they're hard-hearted and selfish and they won't listen. Or they're not open to the Spirit of God. So one reason that preaching doesn't work might be a problem of the people.

Some people suggest that preaching doesn't work because of the preacher. Calvin Miller, in his book *The Sermon Maker*, tells three modern-day parables about a pastor, in order to explain why today's preaching isn't working in the Church. He portrayed the pastor as having a hard heart. The pastor needed to come into a more intimate relationship with Jesus, and then his preaching would have passion again. So, the problem can be the preacher, not the people.

Some people say that we're telling the wrong story. They say, "Stop telling the Americana version of Christianity and start telling the radical call of Jesus. Then preaching will work again."

But I'm going to suggest a different single reason, because I don't think it's any of those three.

I think the reason preaching doesn't work is because it creates the wrong socialization construct. The act of one person's telling a bunch of other people how life is supposed to go is one-way communication; the pastor prepares the message, the pastor delivers the message, and the people just sit there and take it. I don't think preaching is bad, but I think preaching as speechmaking is a fully flawed mechanism. So I'm suggesting this thing called progressional preaching, or dialogical preaching.

Here's how progressional preaching would work: It's like a conversation, a good conversation. I say something and then Tim says something. Now I think of something that I didn't think of before Tim said what he said, and then Joyce says something. Now the three of us have moved on to someplace that we never could have reached on our own. The conversation and the preaching are progressing; they're going somewhere.

It's not question and answer. It's that you have something to say and I have something to say; and when those things come together, we progress, and sometimes we regress. But we're in movement together. I think the truth of God is within you and within me; and when we preach the story of Jesus, it's not speechmaking. Preaching shouldn't be reduced to speechmaking.

Practitioner 4: Going back to what you said earlier, you said that the problem with preaching is that it creates a different what?

Doug: It creates the wrong socialization construct, the wrong socialization pressure. You have to understand, I'm a sociologist and an anthropologist in my B.A. training.

There's nothing wrong with giving a speech on occasion. The problem is the fact that people may go to a church for five years, and over those five years, they'll hear 40 speeches a year, because maybe they'll make it to church 40 times. They're going to hear 200 speeches, but the pastor never hears from them on any of the topics. It's bad not only for the listener but also for the pastor. It's like water hitting rock over and over and over, finally creating sand.

There's nothing wrong with one speech act. The problem is the socialization pressure of saying something over and over and over, and of people's just having to sit there and take it.

A friend of mine, who is a youth pastor of a church, once said to his pastor, "Look, there's this really rich guy, and his kids are in the youth ministry, but he doesn't come to church. What do you think we can do about it?" And do you know how his pastor responded? He said, "Men with that kind of power don't want to come to places to listen to other men tell them how to live their lives." His point was that this rich guy is a hard-hearted person who won't submit himself to the authority of preaching. I think my friend's pastor is right about part of it: The man doesn't want to sit there and listen to someone

My job as a preacher is not to be the voice of God.

tell him how to live his life. But I believe that the reason he doesn't want to is different: He wants to engage in the dialogue about how we're all going to live our lives.

My job as a preacher is not to be the voice of God.

Practitioner 5: So in terms of preparation for the kind of dialogue that we've been talking about—I believe that the Holy Spirit can work through preplanned preparation and speaking—what do you think that looks like?

Doug: I don't fully know, so let me just put a few words around this, because preaching's not all that thrilling to me. In my community, we hold a dialogue group on Tuesday night to look at the part of the Bible that we're going to use the next Sunday night. We create Sunday's topic together in conversation, and then there's an articulation of that in our gathering on Sunday, where it's played with again. My biggest frustration is that we don't include more people in the process. I'm surprised by how many people just like to sit there and take it. It's a form of masochism, and I don't get it.

I IMAGINE A CHURCH THAT SEES ITSELF IN RHYTHMIC HARMONY WITH GOD, NOT SEPARATE FROM GOD.

Doug: Now, I'm going to agenda-ize for a minute. If I could pick one of the topics from the list, it would be this thing of separation from God, rather than rhythm with God—number 1.23.

It's my assumption that there's an awful lot of theology in Christianity that says God has a certain job description and humans have certain job descriptions, and the two shall never meet.

This means that God has an agenda—what He is doing in the world—and that humans have an agenda, but the two never come together. In fact, since God is holy and utterly different from humans, what's on His job description should never be on people's job descriptions. In the Catholic Church, for example, there's this strong belief that we should not interfere with reproduction, because that's God's job description. In some Protestant groups, there's this idea that we shouldn't be involved in genetic research, because that's not the job of humans—it's God's job. God and human beings have different job descriptions.

I happen to think that God invites us to something else entirely. Since we are created as human beings and created in the image of God, the very agenda of God becomes our very agenda. I think that the call of the gospel is that we are invited to become involved in the very agenda of God. The thing that separates the humans from the animals is not that we think and reason and read. The very call and the very distinctiveness of humanity is that we are invited to participate in God's full agenda.

Practitioner 5: I'm glad you're not God.

Doug: Yes, well, I'm in no way assuming that I'm going to become God. What I'm assuming is that whatever God's involved with in the world, I'm to be involved in. Whatever's on God's job description, I'm to participate in. I'm not seeking to become God; I'm seeking to become fully human.

But the understanding that God's agenda is distinct from humanity's agenda doesn't come from Christianity; it is sort of like the Greek, or Hellenistic, understanding of Christianity. Christianity is

not a Western religion of a God who is distinct from humanity; Christianity is an Eastern understanding of a God who dwells with us, the Emmanuel, the God in the Garden.

God's agenda is our agenda, and we invite everyone to participate in it. We don't consider anyone who is working to accomplish the agenda of God to be our competition. We consider those who are trying to destroy the agenda of God to be our competition. We don't compete with other people who are seeking to bring about what God is bringing about. There are already plenty of people seeking to destroy it.

I IMAGINE A CHURCH WITH OPTIMISTIC, CREATIVE AND GREATER IMAGINATION—THE GREATEST FEAR IS THE LOSS OF IMAGINATION.

Practitioner 6: 1.11?

Doug: 1.11. I can imagine a Church with optimistic, creative and greater imagination—the greatest fear is the loss of imagination.

We need to create systems in which we say to people, "You need to hope and dream and imagine." We're called to ask and say, "Couldn't it be?" "What if it was?" and "There it is." So we look around and see the kingdom of God wherever it is active and say, "What if it was?" I would cherish a collection of people who together would ask not only, "Where is the line?" but also, "What are the possibilities?" We should foster it in our children; we should foster it in ourselves; we should foster it in our old people. They should be dreaming dreams and having visions—all people, not just the select people, and with a sense of optimism and growth and life.

Practitioner 6: How do we develop this creativity and imagination without doing something that is used for destructive purposes? Obviously, we're very creative people; but around the world, creativity is often fairly destructive.

Doug: Yeah, we live in a very complex world where the answer to one problem creates its own problems. That is why I am not a true-blue, social-gospel liberal from the 1920s, '30s and '40s. They would say, "If we work hard enough, we will bring about the kingdom of God on Earth." But I would say, "If we work with God well enough, we will create all sorts of other problems that other people are going to have to solve."

There will be a time when this world is going to be recreated. I don't know how that's going to figure out; I don't think it will be in the way that the stories have been told in the twentieth century. So it's true that until then, the answer for today creates the problems of tomorrow. But let that not stop us from trying to provide some answers for today.

Practitioner 7: Do you have any ideas for how we can better handle our creativity, in the sense of constructing something that is going to be beneficial?

Doug: I think we need to stop critiquing people who seek to be creative, just because they're cheesy. I think that's the beginning of the tool set.

I know nothing about art, right? I'm in a community of artists in our church, not because I want to deliver the gospel to them, but because I want them to lead me into a kind of faith that I can't get to on my own. I'm around artists and being led by artists because I'm pathetic, not because I have an answer that I'm trying to download to them. So I don't really know.

And I don't know why artists are so bothered by Thomas Kinkade; but for crying out loud, Thomas Kinkade is not the problem. His work might be cheesy, fine, but there are reasons why people like that stuff. It is to our peril to just write it off as being stupid.

Practitioner 8: Someone may say that there's idealism in the idea that every voice should be included and everybody is given a place. How do we lead then? Do you have a theology of leadership, and what would that look like?

Doug: Here's my theology of leadership, for whatever it's worth. It's really a philosophy of leadership. I think theology is really important, but theology means the study of God and the things of God. So I really have a philosophy of leadership more than a theology of one.

I think that we always have to have people who are leading; they just don't have to be the same people leading all the time. If you walk into a room where the people don't value one person's being a leader, say to that group of people, "How come you don't have a leader?" Whoever answers the question is the leader, right?

Let's just recognize the fact that people lead, but it doesn't have to be the same person all the time, in every area. This is totally my bias: The theological concept of ordination—that one person, as distinct from the rest of the people, is called to have authority in the kingdom of God over a community of people—is an enormous problem. It's not a problem just because the ordained thinks that he or she has the power; it's also because the rest of the people tell the ordained that he or she has that power. The problem is not just in the ordained; it's also in the fact that people keep saying, "Well, that's your job, isn't it, pastor?"

I think there's always someone leading—even multiple people leading—but it doesn't have to be the same person all the time. A void of leadership is as bad as a loving dictatorship. So I'm not trying to suggest that we need a pluralism of leadership, not at all, but we have to recognize that different people can lead us at different periods of time.

We try to have this kind of dialogue in our community, and it helps us a lot. When hundreds of people have to stop for a minute and listen to somebody from their own community, especially someone that they don't really want to listen to, that's the right way to teach a sense of leadership. It's as if they learn to say, "You get to lead me for a while. I'm not necessarily going to go everywhere you want to go, but for a moment I'm going to try it on. I recognize that you may be called by God to take us somewhere right now."

We abuse that kind of thing all the time, because if somebody has an idea, I'm like, "Great, you're in charge." That's not fair. Can't you have an idea without having to be an implementer? Well, not around our place, because we just don't have enough implementers. If you have the slightest hint of an idea, it's like, "You're the president now, right? You're in charge. This is your world to run."

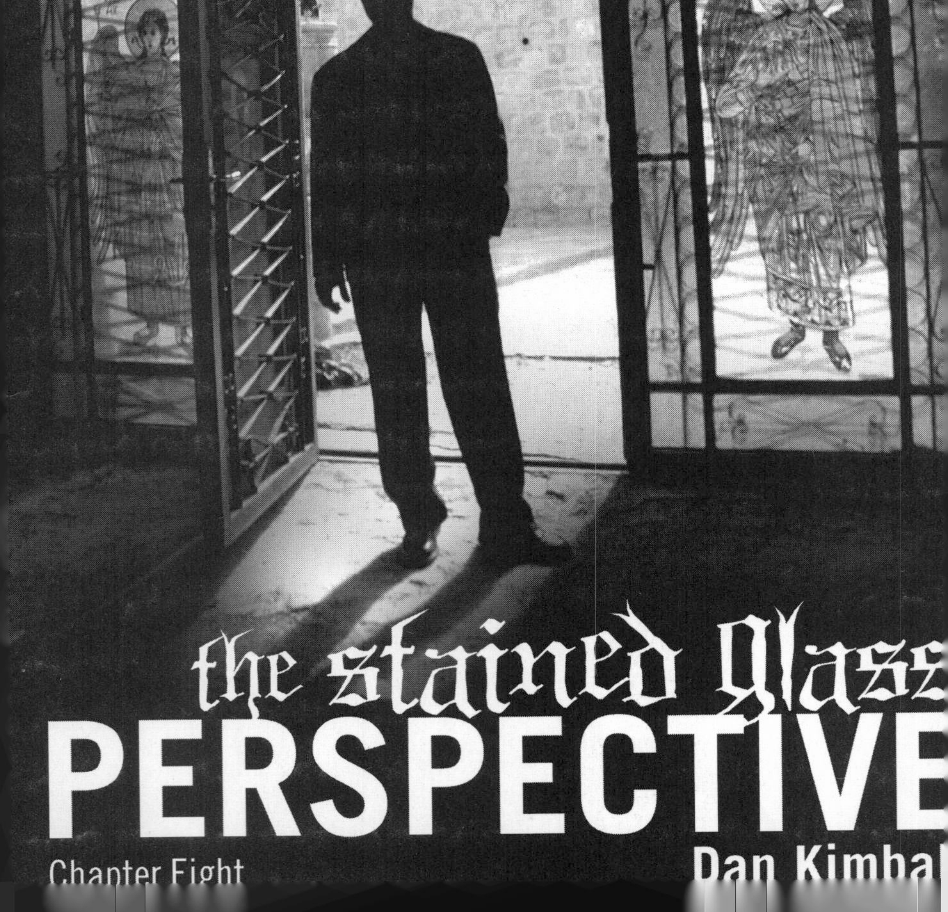

the stained glass PERSPECTIVE

Chapter Eight

Dan Kimball

At a recent gathering, I heard someone say, "We're all starting to agree on the fact that everything in our bones is saying that the Church is undergoing a change." For many of us, we can feel it in our hearts, we can feel it in our guts, and we can feel it in our hair. We just know that the Church and our culture are undergoing rapid change.

We talked years ago and used the "Generation X" phrase, and then we realized that it was more than Gen X. It became "postmodern." And now "postmodern" is almost a bad word because we've misused it and pretty much turned it into a generational issue or style, which is not what postmodernism is. This change is more than a generational thing.

The exciting part is that the emerging church really sees church as mission. Church is no longer just a place that we're supposed to go to. Church is mission, and we're on this mission together. Without that mission, I think that we become inward, we lose ourselves in consumerism, and we forget about the fact that the world is becoming increasingly this way.

What's interesting is that you can get all excited and inspired after reading all these ideas or hearing about art's being used as a wonderful expression of worship, but then you go back—especially for those who are youth pastors—and try to express this to your senior pastor, and you get a blank look. Or maybe you get, "What are you talking about?"

Or you look at an idea like speaking from the center of the room (in the round), and you ask yourself, *How can we start expressing worship in a new way that is unique to our group?* But one of your elders may look at you and say, "What are you talking about?" You might start to wonder to yourself, *Am I crazy? I remember reading about this new thing. I remember experiencing this at a conference. I remember experiencing this at another church. Am I going crazy?* And maybe something doesn't feel right.

Are you trying to reach to the future, recognizing that culture and church are changing, but you're being told that you're crazy?

Once you get infected with this (maybe that's why you're reading this book), the infection starts spreading through your body and into your mind. It's then that you start doing things that concern church, mission, people and almost everything you do differently—even your thought processes start evaluating things differently.

Then, as some of us have been doing for about 10 years, you'll start going through a deconstruction moment when you ask yourself, *What is church? What is ministry? What is theology?*

Recently I was talking to Greg on the phone, and he mentioned Acts 17, which talks about Paul in Athens. Verse 21 says that all who lived in Athens "spent their time doing nothing but talking about and listening to the latest ideas." I believe that for about 10 years, the Church has been in this kind of conversation; we've just been talking and listening, talking and listening.

But it's a wonderful feeling to know that so many of us are now starting to do what Paul did next: He "stood up in the meeting" (v. 22) and gave a very famous speech. He told the Athenians about the God who would invade their lives and about how Jesus, who had been resurrected, also would invade their lives and transform them. In the Church, we're in an interesting time period, in which we need now not to be just talking; we need to be standing up and doing something.

I don't know about your church, but from my travels around the country, I hear the same stories over and over again. People say, "I came back from a meeting [or conference or whatever], and I tried to tell the pastors I'm working with about this change, and they just looked at me like I was crazy. I feel like a Mac in a PC world now."

The question I want to raise here is this: Are you, in your particular church, trying to reach to the future, recognizing that culture and church are changing, but you're being told directly or indirectly that you're crazy?

I'd like to share a little bit from my personal history. I was at the same church for about 13 years, and we recently launched something new called Vintage Faith Church, which I'll share a little about later. I was at a point several years ago when I basically wrote a resignation letter. I had my wife's parents read it over and another pastor on my staff read it over, and then I went into the office of the person to whom I was reporting to tell him that I wouldn't be at his church anymore. I wanted to explain to this person what led up to that decision. And I want to share with you a little bit of this personal journey, simply because you might understand it or relate to it.

I was in this wonderful, fantastic, godly, excellent, beautiful church, which was extremely passionate about God, and I had been there for 13 years. However, when you start thinking differently and you're in a church that is kind of the same and you start saying things like, "Can we have a closet to put art supplies and prayer-station materials in?" you might get an answer like, *"Why* are you using art? And what is a prayer station?"

Or perhaps you say, "Can we build a different stage so that the speaker can be more among everyone, rather than up high away from them?" and many different questions come up like, "What's wrong with this stage? Preachers need to be above everyone on a higher stage."

You may begin speaking about "being the church" instead of "going to church" and get strange looks from the other staff. You may start asking questions about evangelism: "Is the way I have thought of it before still effective, or even right?"

You start asking these kinds of questions and people will start saying constantly, "What's going on here?"

Even in the midst of something that God was blessing, I was getting questioned and even resisted by those I reported to in the church. Instead of celebrating what God was doing, I wondered whether I was going off the deep end and why was I making so many changes. There comes a point when you have to wonder, *Do I leave the church?* I don't know if any of you have had any of these types of conversations, but it seems to be rampant across the country right now.

Just recently I was talking to a guy in ministry at a wonderful, Bible-teaching church. Yet he's quitting, and he's almost about to chuck his faith, because he's had nobody to whom he can say, "I feel like the church is changing, and I don't know what to do." And he thinks *he's* crazy! I kept saying to him, "No, no, no, you're not crazy. You're not crazy!"

ARE YOU EXPERIENCING CHANGES?

Share them with others at www.practitionersbook.com

REFLECT

Do you feel crazy? In what way?

I want to explain something that has been kind of a turning point for me. I got to the point that I was thinking to myself, *What is a pastor anymore?* I just didn't know. But I did know that I didn't like the way pastors tried to control things and to hurt people who wanted to do things differently. Then I thought, *Wait a minute; I'm one of them. I'm one of them!* But what is a pastor? Is a pastor an administrator or a preacher, or is a pastor something else? All of these other questions have come up too, like, What is church? and, What are we doing?

STAINED GLASS

With all this happening and all the tension, I knew I had to get away and think and pray. Our worship leader, who liked to go down to Carmel, California, about 30 miles south of Santa Cruz, told me about a nice, quiet church there. I was feeling like I needed to get centered, so I decided to go. As I went out to my car—a 1966 Mustang—because of the state of mind I was in, all I saw were the little rust spots, and I thought to myself how rust was like pastors and like the Church.

So I got in the car and drove down to Carmel. When I arrived at the chapel, it was fairly dark inside. I'd been there about 10 minutes when a family walked in and took pictures of the place. About 10 minutes later, a person who was yakking really loudly burst in. It was tourist season. My worship leader didn't tell me that this beautiful chapel was a tourist attraction and that people would be coming in the whole time. So I was frustrated about this, about the rust on my car, about pastors—that's what was going on in my head. It was supposed to have been a serene time of seeking God and getting centered, as I thought about change, church and what's going on in culture.

Then another family came in. I decided that I was going to lie down on the floor and hide. So I lay down between the church pews and told myself, *I'm just going to pray until they leave.* As I was praying, a little boy looked in from the aisle and cried, "Daddy, there's a man on the floor!"

I just looked at him and said, "I'm just lying here." It was an awkward little moment, because I didn't know what to do.

Then I thought, *God, I don't know what's up and what's down with the Church. What am I going to do?* I was lying there, and all of a sudden—I'm not exaggerating—the room got incredibly colorful. I was like, *Ahh, something's happening. Maybe Tim LaHaye was right about the Rapture!*

I looked up and there were stained-glass windows on the sides. The sun had just come out and was shining through the stained glass. All the colors brilliantly lit up the room. I had seen the stained glass when I came in, but I didn't really pay attention to it, because it was so dark inside. In the stained glass there were these fairly typical pictures of Jesus, Joseph and Mary coming back from Egypt, but then I started to look closer. My heart was quieting down, and I started to see much more detail in all of the intricate pieces that composed one pane. Then the sun came through the window, and the stained glass became a beautiful picture.

I noticed that these panes depicted individuals from Church history. So I went into the church office and picked up a brochure about the windows. I ended up sitting in the chapel, reading about these people, who lived through different cultural changes throughout history.

I saw a pane that depicted Saint Augustine, who lived from A.D. 354 to 430, a time period when Christianity was becoming accepted and culture as a whole was changing dramatically. Here was a guy who loved God. On the pane, the artist depicted a heart, symbolizing

Augustine's fervent love for Christ. But there also were arrows going through the heart, because Augustine was grieved for his past sins. Augustine is also shown writing, because God used him to pen some beautiful writings to accomplish His purposes in that time of history.

Then I saw a pane depicting a guy named Saint Boniface, who ministered in Germany and lived from around A.D. 673 to 754. Boniface also lived in a changing culture, as in that particular time period, Germany was filled with pagan religions, some of which actually worshiped trees and taught that spirits existed in specific sacred oak trees. So Boniface went out and cut down one of these sacred oak trees to show that it was a false god; then he built a chapel out of the wood to demonstrate that there is only one true God.

In the artist's depiction of Boniface, there are two images. The first image shows Boniface holding an ax, which represents his making a stand when he chopped down that tree. The second image is a sword stabbing through a book, which represents his death. When Boniface was murdered, he had with him a copy of Saint Ambrose's book *The Advantage of Death*, which he revered so much that he lifted it up in the air to prevent the swords from destroying the book when he was murdered.[1] So that's another snapshot of someone in history who struggled and got murdered for the stand that he took.

Then I saw a pane that portrayed Johann Sebastian Bach with an organ. Interestingly enough, Bach lived from 1685 to 1750, during the Enlightenment. In the picture, you can see two Greek letters that mean "Jesus Christ" and the letters that stand for the phrase, "For the glory of God alone." When Bach created his musical pieces, on most all of them he would write, "For the glory of God alone."

As I sat there and looked at the many other people depicted on the panes in this church, I started feeling small. I had this sense that culture changes all the time. We can get so wrapped up in this huge change and how we have to do these different things and the fact that other people don't seem to understand. Then I thought, *What is going on in my heart? At this moment, how would I be pictured on stained glass?* At that moment, if someone created my stained-glass window, I probably wouldn't have looked very happy. I probably would have been pictured with my rusty Mustang, black clouds around me, with an unhappy expression on my face that depicted my dislike of pastors.

That's a pretty sad picture.

I just felt like, *Lord, if You were to capture me now, is that how I'm supposed to be living my life? Even serving You with all my heart?* And it wasn't like I wasn't serving Him.

I sat there and flipped open my Bible. I was looking at the stained glass thinking, *Lord, You created all of these different men and women throughout history, whom You have used for all different types of change in different cultures.* Then I read this passage in Ephesians 2:8: "For it is by grace you have been saved, through faith—and this not from yourselves."

Then I was able to calm down and think, *Oh Lord, thank You—for despite my stain, despite the state of mind and heart that I am currently in, You can still use me and have a purpose for me in this time period and culture.*

I continued reading from Ephesians: "It is the gift of God—not by works, so that no one can boast. For we are God's workmanship, created in Christ Jesus to do good works, which God prepared in advance for us to do" (2:8-10).

God prepared us and gave us a specific mission. God had a specific mission for Bach; He had a mission for Boniface; He had a mission for all these people throughout history; and He has a mission for each of us too.

The word "workmanship" comes from the Greek word *poiema*, from which we get the word "poem."[2] So we can say that God

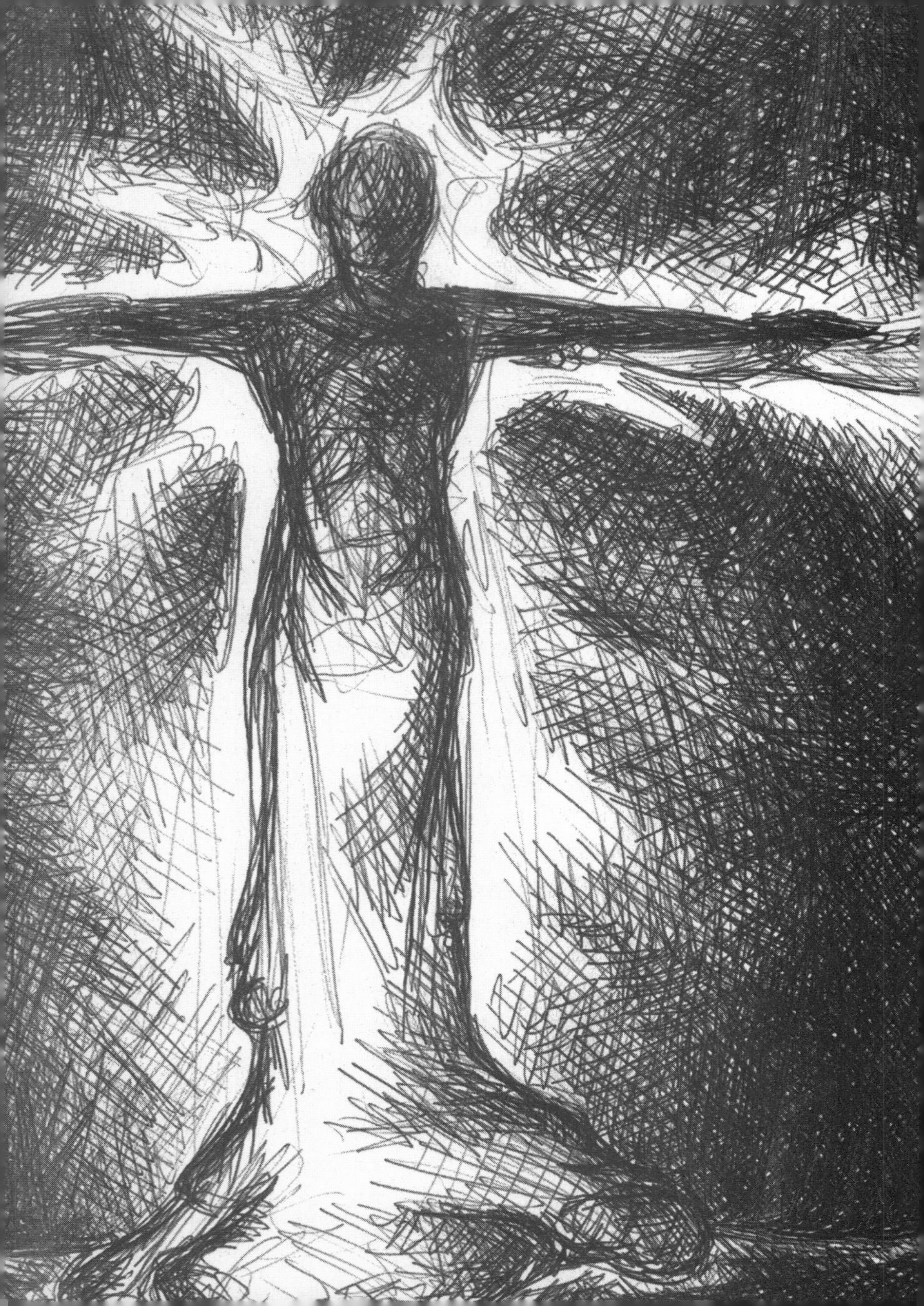

creates each of us as a piece of art, as a piece of poetry. Every one of us is a poem that God writes, something that He has created to be of use for the mission He has given us.

In Ephesians 3:1-9, Paul goes on to talk about his own purpose; and in verse 10, he says something interesting: "His [God's] intent was that now, through *the church*, the manifold wisdom of God should be made known to the rulers and authorities in the heavenly realms, according to his eternal purpose which he accomplished in Christ Jesus our Lord" (emphasis added).

I sat there in the chapel for a long time. As I did, I watched the sun come through the window, I saw the stories on the stained glass, and I examined my heart, putting it all into perspective. We're just in another cultural shift, so this is not the end of the world. Throughout time there have been so many interesting things that have happened, and now we're just in another little glimmer of time.

Then I started thinking about the Church. God chooses us as art, and in this sense we are all broken pieces of stained glass, and He has chosen us for this particular time period. It probably would have been easier to be a pastor or a leader 50 years ago, but we're in this time period, even though we didn't ask to be here. So He assembles us, all of these little fragmented pieces of colored glass, and He puts us together. And then it's not just us, because when I walked into that room, it was dark—but then the sun shined through. It's as if Christ's light shines through the pieces of art and poetry—each of us—on display as the Church to the world. We aren't the light, but we are the stained glass that the light of Jesus shines through.

I just sat there and said to myself, "What is my mission then?" I drew a little diagram of a stained-glass pane and said, "Lord, what I know is that I want Jesus to be at the center." So I drew the word "Jesus" at the center of the paper.

I continued, "And I believe that the Scriptures need to be taught

We aren't the light, but we're the stained glass that the light of Jesus shines through.

to people in a creative way."

Then I drew a Bible around the name "Jesus." And around the Bible I drew a palette, like an artist's palette of colors, and I said, "My passion is to communicate Jesus and the Scriptures in a creative way to a world that's asking questions, seeking and looking." I then drew people's faces and question marks, and arrows moving from the palette out to them.

I continued on, "I also believe that the Church really needs to see itself as the people of God on a mission, not as a building or a weekly meeting. We don't go to church; we are the Church." So I drew a church building with an X through it, and I drew more people, representing that the Church is people, not a building. I completed this sketch of what my stained glass would be, and I continued to sit there and pray.

As I calmed down and sorted through a lot of what I was going through in my church, with all the misunderstandings between the senior pastor and other staff leaders and myself, I began to realize something: We all love God, but maybe we think about ministry and church differently. That doesn't mean one is right and one is wrong. We were just rethinking church and mission for different people groups and cultures. But being in ministry in the same church with different ways of thinking about it can cause clashes. Sadly, poor attitudes and bitterness can creep in as a result. So I spent some time praying and thinking and confessing where I may have developed bitterness or a bad attitude.

As we continue the emerging-church conversation, we need to avoid saying, "Look what they did wrong," but instead say, "May God continue to use them as much as possible while we continue to look at church this other way." We need to advance the emerging church in love, not criticism.

We're at such a great spot in history, on the brink of this incredible spiritual openness. Recently I got a Brian Setzer CD, and he usually sings about drinking, girls and cars. I was looking at my new CD and noticed that the first song is called "Sixty Years." It talks about the idea that we only have 60 years on this planet. The chorus begins like this:

> Nobody wants to talk about it;
> I guess that's true.
> But you'll know, yes you will,
> when your time is through.[3]

As I listened to that song, I was thinking, *What's going on with Brian Setzer?* The next song is called "Drink Whiskey and Shut Up," so I skipped that one. Then I found a song called "St. Jude." I thought, *Wow, what's he talking about here?* The words say things like, "Pray for us, we need some peace." Then they continue,

> If you proclaim the mystery of faith
> You'll be absolved from daily strife
> Through Him, in Him, and within Him
> Springs our eternal life.[4]

When I heard those lyrics, I was just like, *Huh?* So now I have no idea what Setzer believes—none. But he's singing about Jesus. What a fantastic thing! We'd better realize that people are beginning to be open to Jesus and open to spiritual things. We need to join this grand adventure, because we're in a fantastic period in history.

People are becoming open to Jesus, and we'd better not let our own opinions or disagreements get in the way of the broader mission. I just pray that as the emerging church we would guard our hearts, because we're each pieces of stained glass, put together uniquely by God and put on display for all these people to see. Everyone is different and we're all stained, but He still uses us. For me, I needed to confess my bitterness and admit I was hurt, but also realize it wasn't intentional. The leaders in the church were just used to ministry a certain way, and I was trying to change ministry to a different way. But we all are on the same mission, just in different ways, like I saw in the different examples on the stained glass in the chapel.

I never turned in that resignation letter. I went into that office to meet with the pastor I reported to, and I just looked at him and thought, *He's a really good guy.* All of the disagreements we were having weren't about Jesus. We just viewed church and ministry differently, because we are passionate about reaching different kinds of people. So we talked and then we struggled; we talked and then we struggled. We prayed together. And eventually we decided that we should start a new church, taking the ministry ideas I was experimenting with and giving them full freedom. We ended up launching this church with the full blessing and great support from the church I was a part of.

In the emerging church, we need to recognize that there will be all types of ministry and churches. There isn't a right or wrong way; there will be a myriad of expressions of church. But it may be hard to make change if you are in an existing church. Maybe your mission is to make change in your church. Maybe your mission is to start a new church. But remember that we are all on this mission together. It took me a day in a chapel looking at stained-glass images of people throughout history to realize this. All of those people were different from each other, but they all had the same

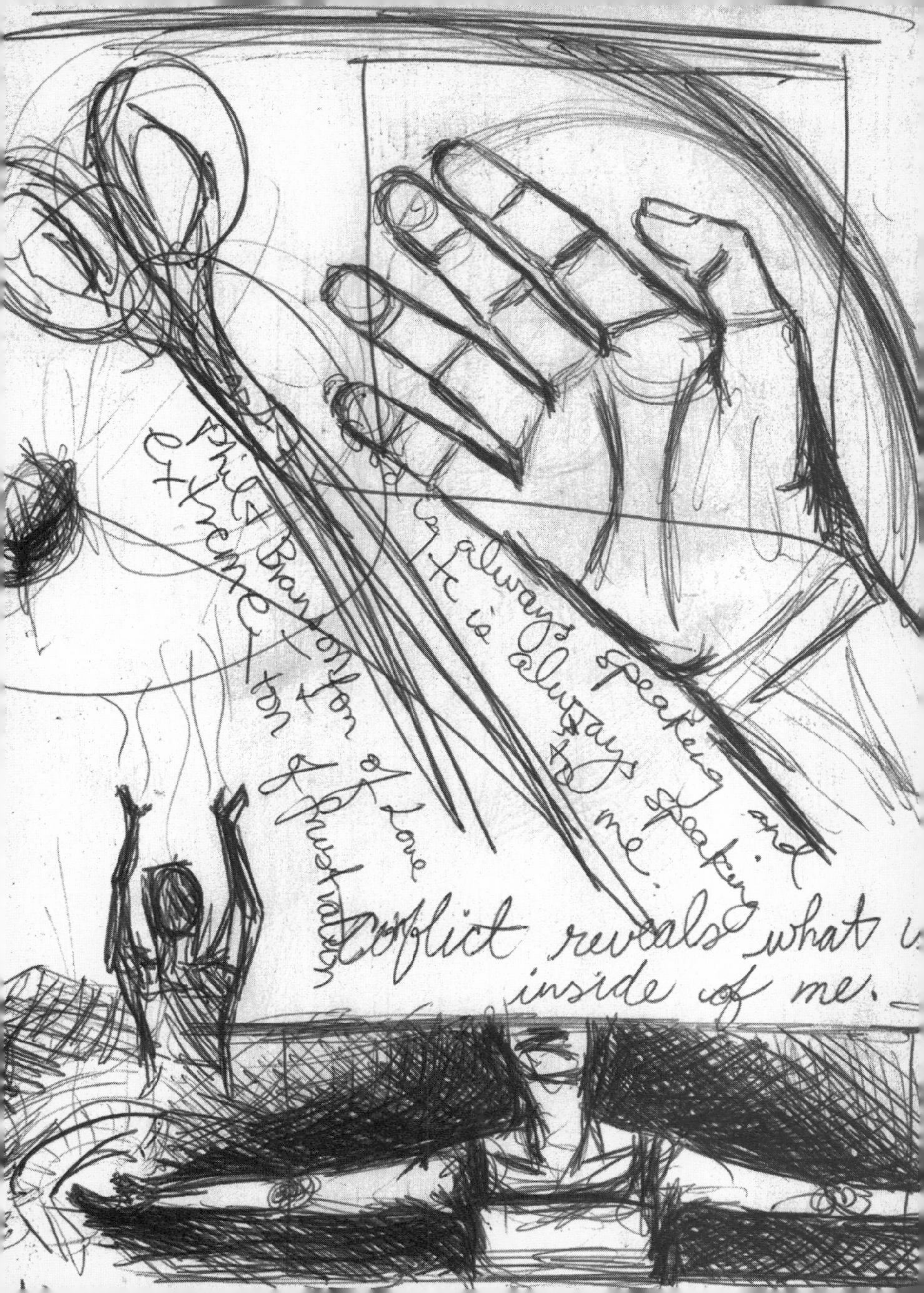
is always speaking and
He is always speaking to me.
Phil 4 Branton ton of Love
extreme ton of frustration
Coflict reveals what i
inside of me.

ultimate goal of seeing Jesus be made known to others and walking in His ways.

Picture what your stained-glass window would look like right now. Maybe you don't like what it would portray, but what could it be in your future? You can ask God to shape you and change you for whatever it is that He may want. What specific things would be on your new stained glass? God has created you for a unique mission.

And when you talk to someone later about the thoughts you're thinking or the things you're reading, and this person looks at you funny and thinks you're crazy, what you can think is, *No, I'm not, because there are many others just like me.*

ON THE NEXT PAGE, TAKE SOME TIME TO CRAFT YOUR STAINED-GLASS WINDOW.

NOTES

1. Francis Mershman, "St. Boniface," *The Catholic Encyclopedia, Volume II* (New York: Robert Appleton Company, 1907). http://www.newadvent.org/cathen/02656a.htm (accessed June 15, 2005).
2. *Merriam-Webster's Collegiate Dictionary,* 11th ed., s.v. "poem."
3. Brian Setzer, "Sixty Years," *Nitro Burnin' Funny Daddy,* © 2003 Surf Dog (Ada).
4. Brian Setzer, "St. Jude," *Nitro Burnin' Funny Daddy,* © 2003 Surf Dog (Ada).

4576 03/02/99 14:26:45
GA(LMP)=22W5D P80 NP C364

chapter nine

LET US BEGIN

Pete Greig

God was reconciling the world to himself in Christ.
2 Corinthians 5:19

The practitioners in this book represent a broad array of experience; they champion important ideas and dare to pose disruptive questions for the emerging culture. There are so many threads of thought—so many colors of opinion—that the whole could seem somewhat chaotic and the natural human tendency would be to try to tidy things up. But if the quantum physicists are correct, then diverse and chaotic conversations like these are in fact a divine loom on which God weaves some of his most glorious patterns. Provided we love Him and align ourselves with His purposes, we can relax in the certainty that He is busy reconciling all things to himself, lovingly ensuring that all things work together for the greater good (see Romans 8:28).

So that's why I don't want to untangle the threads of thought in this book too much. I don't want to explain and reconcile everything, because I'm convinced that a little apparent conflict, or tension, is a thoroughly healthy thing. Instead I want to examine and explore this knotted ball of colored threads, tracing the shapes they are weaving until we find a few of the patterns that God Himself may be creating from the chaos, as well as the beauty that He may be weaving from the mess of our relationships.

ATTRACTIVE DIVERGENCE

We have probably all been unsettled by some of the ideas voiced in this book. Perhaps you have been disturbed by the opinions of controversialists like Spencer Burke, Doug Pagitt or that subversive hippy Greg Russinger! But—and this is the fun part—each one of us has almost certainly been disturbed, offended and helped by *different* parts of the same book. And should you care to read *Practitioners* again next year, you may find yourself disturbed, offended, encouraged or bored by an entirely different set of pages from the ones that have had such an impact on you this time round. We are different people from different backgrounds at different places on our journeys toward God. Who, then, brings us together in churches, conferences and conversations like the ones reflected in this book? Who makes beauty out of the chaotic fractals of our apparent divergence? It is Christ who brings us together. There can be no other.

But now let's switch from the Sunday School question, *Who* brings us together? to the altogether subtler enquiry, *What* brings us together? What is it that gives us a common language? What are we actually practitioners of? And while I'm at it, what on earth does it mean to be "voices within the emerging culture"? (That's what the cover of this book purports us to be!)

First—in answer to this question of *what* brings us together—let me say that I hope we are not meeting because of marketing. I hope it's deeper than the cover design and more scattered than a single brand, personality or set of permissions. I hope—I think—we are meeting because we are all asking the same sets of questions and we are doing so with a certain amount of insecurity and vulnerability: We are wondering what the *Missio Dei*—the great salvation plan of the Trinity—actually looks like in practice. We are wondering what it requires of us here in contemporary culture. (Of course, "contemporary" is not about fashion. "Contemporary" is simply the bewildering present reality within which we find ourselves set down and raised up as followers of Jesus.)

It is because we are asking these questions—from many different starting points—that we come together *in Christ* to wonder what He might be saying, where He might be living and how He might be thinking if He were right here and right now. Which, of course, He is. And this gives the whole enterprise a dimension of great hope, because we are not asking our questions in order to *access* the mission of God but to *participate* in it! This means that when we debate and disagree, when we explore and experiment *in Christ*, our questions and conclusions are an expression (perhaps even a progression) of the salvation story, as Christ mysteriously reconciles the world to Himself in our time and, even more mysteriously, as He decides to do it through people like us. Together, as voices within a culture (that has been dexterously lumbered with this title "emerging"), we are actively exploring *a very big idea indeed:* the idea that God's strategy on Earth is centered on missional communities and that we are called to participate in such fellowships, reflecting and incarnating both the mission of Christ and the Trinitarian community of Christ right here, right now, on Earth as it is in heaven.

MISSIONAL COMMUNITY

If you too aspire to be a practitioner of truly Christlike friendships that pulse with His heartbeat for the poor and the lost, then you are already part of this conversation. You probably also have been entrusted with some part of the revelation that God wants to bring, so please find ways of speaking up! Together we are attempting to turn "church" into a verb as well as a noun. We are trying to build communities with the unashamed agenda of expressing the eternal mission of God in space and time. No wonder we all have questions!

In the online magazine of the Presbyterian Assembly of America, Rev. Dr. Clark D. Cowden provides a helpful summary of the ethos of the contemporary missional-community movement of which we are a part:

> The missional church movement realizes that we are no longer chaplains to a Christian culture. We must be a missionary people in our land. Every congregation needs to be cross-cultural missionaries to its own community. We must move from the mindset that the church is a provider of religious services to Christian consumers to the shaper of apostolic people on a mission to a fallen world.[1]

And the communities to which we are called to be missionaries are changing quickly as well.

Such a transitional era is both exciting and dangerous for Christian orthodoxy. Prejudices and pillars of the old order are falling. The lightning has struck, and forest fires are bringing down some of the great oaks of the past 300 years. The wooded landscape we knew is changing for good—or maybe for bad. Who can say? But amidst the embers of nostalgia, amidst the smoke and confusion, we can be sure that we shall discover a new, fertile mission field for the old, old gospel.

PETER'S APOSTOLIC PARADIGM SHIFT

At such times we must draw more from the apostolic traditions of Scripture than we do from the trends of transitional culture. So let's now turn to study a similar era in which the Church had to navigate a paradigm shift every bit as dangerous and exciting as the one we are experiencing today. Acts 10 reads,

> At Caesarea there was a man named Cornelius, a centurion in what was known as the Italian Regiment. He

> and all his family were devout and God-fearing; he gave generously to those in need and prayed to God regularly. One day at about three in the afternoon he had a vision. He distinctly saw an angel of God, who came to him and said, "Cornelius!" Cornelius stared at him in fear. "What is it, Lord?" he asked. The angel answered, "Your prayers and gifts to the poor have come up as a memorial offering before God. Now send men to Joppa to bring back a man named Simon who is called Peter. He is staying with Simon the tanner, whose house is by the sea" (vv. 1-6).

I find this amusing: Cornelius got road directions from an angel. Admittedly the directions were a bit vague, but they were certainly better than anything my wife ever supplies. Anyway, I digress.

> When the angel who spoke to him had gone, Cornelius called two of his servants and a devout soldier who was one of his attendants. He told them everything that had happened and sent them to Joppa (Acts 10:7-8).

If this were a movie, the scene would now transition from the house of Cornelius to that of Simon the Tanner. Maybe one of those subtitles would come up on the screen in Courier font: "JOPPA: NOON THE NEXT DAY."

Amidst the embers of nostalgia, amidst the smoke and confusion, we can be sure that we shall discover a new, fertile mission field for the old, old gospel.

> About noon the following day as they were on their journey and approaching the city, Peter went up on the roof to pray. He became hungry and wanted something to eat, and while the meal was being prepared, he fell into a trance. He saw heaven opened and something like a large sheet being let down to earth by its four corners. It contained all kinds of four-footed animals, as well as reptiles of the earth and birds of the air. Then a voice told him, "Get up, Peter. Kill and eat." "Surely not, Lord!" Peter replied. "I have never eaten anything impure or unclean." The voice spoke to him a second time, "Do not call anything impure that God has made clean." This happened three times (Acts 10:10-16).

Presumably, Peter managed to say something stupid the second time as well. We don't know. You can imagine Jesus up there in heaven, saying to the Holy Spirit, "He does this. He always says stupid stuff. Remember the time he offered to build a campsite for Elijah, Moses and me? And the time he tried to talk me out of the Cross? You're probably going to have to say it to him three times." And so, of course, the Holy Spirit did.

> Immediately the sheet was taken back to heaven. While Peter was wondering about the meaning of the vision, the men sent by Cornelius found out where Simon's house was and stopped at the gate. They called out, asking if Simon who was known as Peter was staying there. While Peter was still thinking about the vision, the Spirit said to him, "Simon,

> three men are looking for you. So get up and go downstairs" (Acts 10:16-20).

God had to prompt Peter to go answer the door. His visitors were downstairs, ringing the doorbell—"Ding dong!" Perhaps it was because Peter was so engrossed in prayer that God had to say,

> "Peter, hello? The door? Wake up!" God continued, "Do not hesitate to go with them, for I have sent them." Peter went down and said to the men, "I'm the one you're looking for. Why have you come?" The men replied, "We have come from Cornelius the centurion. He is a righteous and God-fearing man, who is respected by all the Jewish people. A holy angel told him to have you come to his house so that he could hear what you have to say." Then Peter invited the men into the house to be his guests. The next day Peter started out with them, and some of the brothers from Joppa went along. The following day he arrived at Caesarea. Cornelius was expecting them and had called together his relatives and close friends. As Peter entered the house, Cornelius met him and fell at his feet in reverence. But Peter made him get up. "Stand up," he said, "I am only a man myself." Talking with him, Peter went inside and found a large gathering of people. He said to them: "You are well aware that it is against our law for a Jew to associate with a Gentile or visit him. But God has shown me that I should not call any man impure or unclean" (Acts 10:20-27).

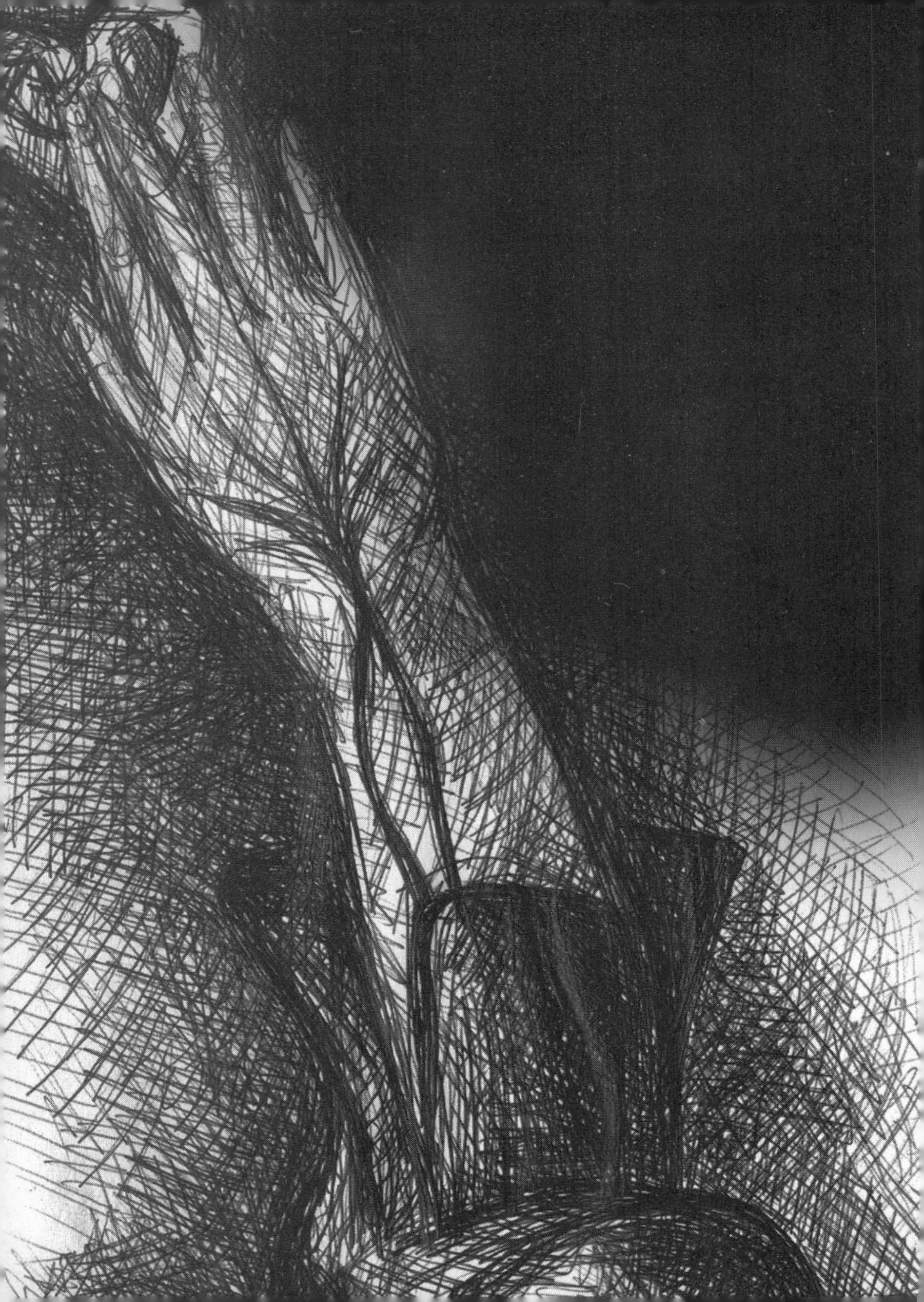

I SHOULD NOT CALL ANY MAN UNCLEAN

I long for the day when every single person who dares to use the word "Christian" of himself or herself would say, "God has shown me that I should not call any man impure or unclean." Imagine a church that refuses to label a man impure or unclean just because he smokes or wears tattoos, recognizing that the Holy Spirit may be moving more powerfully in his life than in their own. Conversely, imagine a church that refuses to call a woman clean or pure just because she has a fish sticker on her car and a Keith Green CD in her stereo. Do I dare take this further? Is God wanting to show us that we should never call any man impure or unclean simply because his sexual temptations are oriented differently from our own or because his politics are different? What would happen if Republican Christians and Democrat Christians stopped throwing allegations of unrighteousness at each other just long enough to confess, "Christ in you, the hope of glory" (Colossians 1:27)? Do we dare to believe that God can move righteously in those who defile our cultural preferences and appall our spiritual sensibilities? Is our God big enough? Does the Cross reach far enough?

In Acts 10, God called Peter to take a quantum leap in order to discover the reality of His purposes in the Gentiles. It was to be a shattering paradigm shift, violating cultural and theological convictions that Peter would have taken in with his mother's milk; but the mission of God depended upon a fundamental alteration in Peter's worldview.

Note, however, that God's new revelation—while shattering—was utterly in tune with the message of Scripture, hidden though it was to many of the contemporary Jews. Having been called as a light to the Gentiles, the Israelites should never have become so prejudiced and blinkered to the possibility of God's grace for other nations.

I am not advocating a sort of enshrined tolerance, in which we refuse to label anything or anyone in the culture impure or unclean out of niceness or cowardice. Sin is sin, and we should not be afraid to name it. However we must also have the courage to acknowledge that God's goodness and grace know no bounds.

My conviction is that all human beings—whether or not they call themselves Christians—are made in the image of God and therefore carry some semblance of the Creator and some capacity to be used for His purposes. It would be foolish to harden our hearts to such a possibility.

As Peter learned that day, we must be very careful before labeling human beings, who are loved by God and made in His image, as unclean or impure. Jesus Himself cautioned us to remove the plank from our own eyes before pointing out the splinter in another's (see Matthew 7:5). Let us treat all people with respect and approach culture with a measure of optimism and humility. Such a posture does not make us universalists. Christ alone is the way to the Father. Salvation is only in and through His life, death and resurrection. In a time of paradigm shift, it is important to hold on to such creedal absolutes—especially in an era that so hates any form of exclusivity.

But as well as holding on to our absolutes, in a time of change it is also important to realize that some of our most deeply treasured securities are soon to be unmasked as simply wrong. We need courage, humility and good friendships in order to know which new ideas are embedded in the timeless truth of Scripture and which ones need to change. For William Wilberforce, living 1,800 years after Peter, at a time when most Christians could still defend slavery using proof texts from the Bible, it took great courage, humility and friendship to find the message of emancipation and equality embedded in the message of Scripture. When such new revelations come to us from God in times of change, they always confirm the core message of Scripture—and never contravene it.

Peter was certainly in such a moment of scriptural revelation, resulting in cultural violation, as he stepped into the house of a Gentile for the first time in his life.

> Peter went inside and found a large gathering of people. He said to them: "You are well aware that it is against our law for a Jew to associate with a Gentile or visit him. But God has shown me that I should not call any man impure or unclean. So when I was sent for, I came without raising any objection. May I ask why you sent for me?" (Acts 10:27-29).

Cornelius recounted to Peter the remarkable tale of his angelic visitation and the instructions that he had received.

> Then Peter began to speak: "I now realize how true it is that God does not show favoritism but accepts men from every nation who fear him and do what is right" (vv. 34-35).

Peter went on to recount the story of Jesus in what we might consider a very conventional way; almost a classical "gospel preach." At times of transition, we discover afresh the eternal and universal relevance of the gospel of Jesus Christ, as appropriate to the new age that is dawning as to the one that has died.

Then something supernatural interrupted Peter's sermon:

> While Peter was still speaking these words, the Holy Spirit came on all who heard the message. The circumcised believers who had come with Peter were astonished that the gift of the Holy Spirit had been poured out even on the Gentiles. For they heard them speaking in tongues and praising God. Then Peter said, "Can anyone keep these people from being baptized with water? They have received the Holy Spirit just as we have." So he ordered that they be baptized in the name of Jesus Christ. Then they asked Peter to stay with them for a few days (vv. 44-48).

MISSIONAL THEMES FOR SEASONS OF CHANGE

In Acts 10 we see many of the themes that have been discussed in this book; practices that are important to missional community, especially in seasons of change.

- *Active engagement with the poor* (see vv. 2,22).
- *Commitment to prayer* (see vv. 2-3,9).
- *A fusion of prayer and justice* (see v. 4).
- *Mysticism.* For example, an angel appeared; Cornelius and Peter saw strange visions; and a group of people spontaneously started to speak in tongues and see strange visions (see vv. 3,9-10,44-46).
- *Holistic spirituality*. God is bigger than every box we try to put Him in (see vv. 15,34-35).

- *Hospitality*. Significantly, it all began with Peter, who was a guest in Simon the tanner's home. Peter received a vision of a feast; a banquet that should have looked attractive, but actually seemed repellent. Peter then offered his surprise guests a bed for the night. They must surely have spent time just talking, relaxing, eating and even laughing that night. When Peter nervously crossed the threshold of Cornelius' home, both men quickly moved beyond their initial religious postures of preaching (Peter) and worshipping (Cornelius) in order to share conversation, food and hospitality. After this seismic encounter, Peter stayed on for several days at Cornelius' house (see vv. 23,48). I can imagine Peter's waking up the next morning in a Gentile bed for the first time in his life and wondering what he should eat for breakfast. Or maybe he went into the bathroom inquisitively to look around.
- *Mission*. More than anything, there is mission at the heart of this passage. There is God's mission in response to Cornelius' prayers; there is Peter, traveling as a missionary to tell the story of Jesus; and then, as a result, there is baptism in water and baptism in the Spirit (see vv. 4,34-48).

INTENTIONAL AND RELATIONAL

My wife, Samie, and I currently live in extended family with a guy called Paul and his wife, Rachel, and, of course, our two kids. This year, we decided not to have a TV, but we soon discovered how easy it is to invent replacements. For example, someone recently gave us a cuckoo clock; and as a result, Paul and I, on the hour, every hour, go sit on the couch and wait for the little bird to come out. When it does, we stand and cheer and then just get on with whatever we were doing before. It's really sad.

Then someone gave us a Ping-Pong table. So Paul and I dove into this really competitive weeklong table-tennis contest, and he beat me every time. It was "Best of three!" and "Best of five!" Guys like to interact that way, and we were yelling and screaming and blaming our paddles and the height of the table for every missed point.

On one occasion, Samie and Rachel were sitting there watching until Paul and I retired from the field of battle to watch the cuckoo clock. As we were sitting there, waiting for the cuckoo, we heard our wives pick up the paddles and start to play. We began to hear laughter coming from the other room.

Eventually the cuckoo did his thing, and we returned to the table tennis, asking our wives who had won their game.

They just giggled, "Oh, we don't know."

They didn't know who had won?!

"But guess what?" they said with evident satisfaction. "We had a rally of 35 shots—35 times over the net! You guys, we watched, and you never once had it over the net more than 4 times, and we," they said proudly, "we managed 35!"

It was an interesting caricature of the difference between the male and the female approaches to life. Of course, there is a place and a time for both the competitive and the cooperative, the intentional and the relational. To be missional people, we must marry the intentional and the relational.

I have a good number of deep friendships, and I like nothing better than hanging out with these people. But if my friends never want to do anything other than hang around—if there's never any scheming and dreaming—I confess I quickly get bored. Conversely, I'm a natural ideas man—a visionary. I'm always getting excited about cool things we could do. But "we" is the operative word—if my friends don't want to come with me in pursuit of my latest adventure, I quickly lose my heart for the vision too.

However, when the vision and the friendship combine— when friends dream, and vision becomes an adventure of deep camaraderie—then I am at my happiest. I think that's why a book or a movie like *The Lord of the Rings* has a sort of primal resonance, because it's driven by this idea of camaraderie, conspiracy, friendship, adventure, safety and, yet, risk.

Jesus had three years to save the planet, and yet He had time to tell stories and to befriend strangers and to turn His followers into lifelong friends.

I don't think I'm alone. I think God wired us this way to marry the intentional and the relational, the missional and the communal. Some of us will be more biased toward one than toward the other, but as communities we are called to be both apostolic and pastoral, directional and relational, visionary and fun.

In the Gospels, we see that Jesus was both intentional and relational. But although He had an agenda, the Lord never pursued purpose in a way that functionalized or dehumanized people. He had time to play with children and to attend parties. He had time to cook breakfast on a beach and to go camping and to pray regularly. Jesus had three years to save the planet, and yet He had time to tell stories and to befriend strangers and to turn His followers into lifelong friends. Jesus had a plan and a purpose, but the heart of this strategy centered on a surprisingly small number of deep friendships with a remarkably unimportant group of people.

TO SHAPE HISTORY

In this section, I want to introduce some ideas about shaping history. In my book *The Vision and the Vow*, I explore these ideas further and apply them to developing a Rule of Life.

The German philosopher Hegel once delivered a very famous series of lectures in Berlin. In these lectures he outlined the two prevailing theories about how history gets shaped.

1. *The World-Spirit Theory*. History is shaped by impersonal forces such as dialectical materialism and a quasi-religious idea of fate.
2. *The World-Leader Theory*. History is shaped by heroic leaders, such as Alexander the Great and Abraham Lincoln, and by the antihero type of leader, such as Hitler.

Christians often fall into the trap of believing that history is indeed only shaped by the impersonal manifestation of the power and the will of God (i.e., the world-spirit theory), which lends a kind of impersonal inevitability to everything; or by the world-leader theory, which leaves us pinning all our prayers on the idea of another great leader like Billy Graham or a Christian president who will change everything.

Hegel was right in that history is indeed shaped by these two forces. We'd be stupid if we thought that the forces of economics or personalities do not change things. Yet I believe there's a third force shaping history, which has a very great deal to teach us as we seek to develop missional communities.

That force is what one commentator describes as the power of *faithful minorities*. It's the power of two or three gathered in the name of Jesus (see Matthew 18:20). Margaret Mead, the respected anthropologist, put it like this:

> Never doubt that a small group of thoughtful, committed citizens can change the world; indeed, it's the only thing that ever has.[2]

Aged 30, Jesus had three years to save the planet and what did He do? He built friendships with a group of thoughtful, committed citizens. They were intentional friendships, and we still live with the implications of those friendships today.

As we gather together with our friends and commit ourselves to intentional relationships in the name of Jesus, we can creatively subvert the prevalent values of society. In fact Jesus showed that such faithful minorities can be the most effective way of changing history.

The Celtic people had the phrase *cymbrogi*, which literally means "companions of the heart." My approach to transformation now is to seek out my cymbrogi. Where are my companions of the heart, with whom I can build relationship and dream? They may well be the key to the purposes of God inherent in missional community.

LET US BEGIN

In this chapter, I have attempted to trace a number of the themes of this book by exploring the purpose and the power of missional communities. The purpose is, of course, the mission of God; and in Acts 10 we found some helpful keys to unlock God's purposes in a season of accelerated change. We have also explored the power of intentional friendship to make history.

The writer of the letter to the Hebrews prays that God would "equip you with everything good for doing his will" (13:21). This is a book by practitioners for practitioners about the practical realities of being missionaries within an emerging culture. Our aim is to engage and equip you with everything good for doing God's will.

Some Christians are content to spend their time networking and blogging, researching and imagining, but we are called to something altogether more practical. While I have been writing and you have been reading, the poor have been getting poorer and our neighbors have learned little of Jesus. There is work for us to do, people for us to see, problems for us to solve; and if this book has enabled you to do that more effectively, then it has been worthwhile.

Saint Francis of Assisi, who was arguably one of the most Christlike and joyful personalities since Christ himself, achieved incredible things with his life. Living in poverty, he preached the gospel passionately and joyfully. He brought renewal to the Church through his Franciscan order of missional communities. By anyone's standards, Saint Francis was a practitioner, an achiever, a revolutionary voice within an emerging culture. One might expect such a man, in his latter years, to issue a sigh of weary satisfaction and to find old age cushioned by a worthy sense of fulfillment. It is all the more remarkable, therefore, to discover that the final words of so great a missionary were in fact these:

> Let us begin, my brothers, for up to now we have done but little.[3]

Like Saint Francis, we long, in our generation, to return to the gospel with such power that we somehow participate in the renewal of the Church, the liberation of the poor and the evangelization of the world. But of course it is easy to "grow weary and lose heart"

(Hebrews 12:3) when things get tough or to become self-satisfied when things appear to have gone well. But in spite of such temptations to mediocrity, the apostolic pilgrim cannot rest in a foreign land. Looking to the future, some of us, like Saint Francis, may not have long to live. That being the case, "let us begin." Whatever we see in the rearview mirror, let's fix our eyes on Jesus. Let us begin and let us keep beginning for the rest of our lives until, at last, life itself begins.

NOTES

1. Clark D. Cowden, "The Missional Church/Missional Presbytery Project," *Perspectives*, November 2002. http://www.pcusa.org/oga/perspectives/nov-frame.htm (accessed June 14, 2005).
2. Margaret Mead, quoted at *Thinkexist.com.* http://en.thinkexist.com/search/searchQuotation.asp?search=never+doubt+that+a+thoughtful (accessed on June 15, 2005).
3. St. Francis of Assisi, quoted in Thomas of Celano, *Thomas of Celano's First Life of St. Francis of Assisi*, trans. Christopher Stace (London: Society for Promoting Christian Knowledge, 2000), p. 103.

CHAPTER TEN Voices

JOURNAL ENTRIES
Si Johnston

After traveling the many landscapes and cultures within the U.K., London became the destination for what I'll record here.

The context is that after a couple of years spent working with students in deprived urban areas of the city, I got involved in resurrecting a near derelict church building in the heart of London. Our dream? To create a 24/7 Prayer center, becoming a resource for holistic Christian mission and spirituality.

My declared hand is that I'm 29, single, northern Irish, educated, driven, and a connoisseur of Asian food and sports of many flavors.

The following passages are a recorded series of four chronologically random journal entries to give you a glimpse into the day-to-day life of mission in London. Each vignette is relayed as I wrote it and only differs in the sense that I've changed some names and given each a heading that might at least serve to frame the excerpt for easier reading.

Stability in the Chaos

I've double booked three times today. Oh for a personal assistant! My day began with a breakfast and discussion of life with a journalist. How does he succeed in his job when his brief is to write—for the benefit of millions of voyeurs who clearly have a thinner existence than they care to admit—near fabrications about the lives of people he doesn't actually know? God knows. I wish I'd backed out of this one and gone to the church planning meeting. Helping other travelers with the ethics of urban living in their attempt to beat out a path of faithfulness is too often beyond me. No moral instability here though; it's an earnest question seeking an earnest answer. It reminds me of my time selling cars—persuading old ladies that they needed to buy a new car when I knew that if they managed to suck the next seven days out of our calendar year, they'd be doing well. Those days have passed, and even with several college degrees (including theology), somehow I'm supposed to have transitioned from used car salesman to purveyor of sage wisdom.

Fortunately, someone once said, "Love the Lord your God with all you've got, and your neighbor as yourself." A statement par excellence. I guess my purpose is simply to help the journalist and everyone else wrap the story of their lives around those words. Just as the development of that internal framework we call the skeleton enabled mobility not yet witnessed on planet Earth, so this truth, when buried deep within the complex structure of humanity, might enable the journalist and all of us to move in ways we haven't yet discovered. What does it mean for him to love his neighbor, for me to love God or, in the big picture, for our world to basically be neighborly toward one another and to the ultimate Neighbor, once evicted?

Scooters, Sandcastles and the Annunciation

After a morning with Ian (a manic depressive and clinical schizophrenic), too many e-mails, a brief discussion about youth work and more news of divorce, I took off to my bolt-hole. Tucked up amongst some Italian scooters in London's best-kept secret—The Scooter Café—I eeked out some time to read. Reading: an almost forgotten pastime for me now (*The Lithium Project* is playing in the background—bolt-holes don't get any better than this). John Caputo discusses the connection between Mary's response to the angel Gabriel

and the fact that with God, amazing things, even incredible things, might just happen:

> **GABRIEL**. Mary, you're going to bring forth a child.
> **MARY**. What on God's green Earth are you talking about? I guarantee, that's impossible.
> **GABRIEL**. Don't worry, nothing will be impossible with God.
> **MARY**. Here I am.

Well done, Mary. Here is a woman of substance being eavesdropped on a millennia later by a man of questionable substance hidden amongst stylish Italian metal. Why is it so difficult to stand with Mary and say, "God, bring it on!" Rhetorical. Because building the Kingdom feels like building sand castles on the beach at Waimea Bay and never failing to see that they don't last longer than a single tidal cycle. And yet, we return day after day to once again watch the highly destructive swells of neurological misfires in Ian, as the riptides of drugs and lovelessness and relational rot seemingly undo everything. "God, it's bloody impossible" and "Mary, how did you say that? If only Eve had been the woman legacy leaver for women!"

I guess it's the incremental gains—unseen acts, less-than-sensational gestures, and conversations—that are significant. Are these the more standard fare for us than the 36 miracles mentioned throughout Jesus' three-year stint? Does the miracle not lie in the fact that it's the fragile, diminishing posse who, in spite of the fact that the steps back seem to outnumber the steps forward, somehow keeps . . . going, keeps . . . believing, keeps . . . hoping?

Nah, that's impossible . . .

Time to leave The Scooter Café. On the way out, I meet Meister Eckhardt, who whispers to me, "Spirituality is not to be learned in flight from the world, by fleeing from things to a place of solitude (or scooters); rather, you must learn to maintain an inner solitude regardless of where you are or who you are with. You must learn to penetrate things and find God there."

So from now on, with Mary, I must answer from that place deep inside, which suggests that the emerging future is so impossible that all I can do is say, "Yes, bring it on . . . Yah-weh."

Easter Dinner with an MTV Buddhist

Some friends asked me to come for a "simple" Easter dinner today. With a warm welcome, I entered and was immediately asked to regale stories of growing up in northern Ireland. After our meal, the conversation went to the issue of religion. The Christians, apparently now feeling some solidarity because a bona fide vicar had arrived, began to "demysticize" my friend Jake's well-thought-through convictions about Buddhism over and against a choice for Christian faith. Hey, the guy has asked me to his house for dinner; I was probably best off not ratting on him.

"So Jake, what's it like working for MTV?" There was no point; this was now a war of attrition between religious takes, a microcosm of that which is happening all across the Western world. Where would I stand? I decided not to take a stand but to occupy the middle space and arbitrate. Interestingly, with Jake's ability to quote endless authors and philosophers, I wanted to hear more from him, but this wasn't to be; his voice was a lone voice in a melee of certainty. And rather than fight fire with fire, Jake had learned, clearly, to live and let live, all in the interests of familial and global peace.

What Would Jesus Do? Who Would Jesus Deconstruct? The earnest Christians on my left or the "erroneous Buddhist" on my right?

Jesus didn't always feel the need to walk out with another scalp, and on this occasion, neither did I. Jake's intensity and hunger for something that made sense of his world were attractive. In fact, it made much more sense than the passionately argued egocentric Christian worldview corner. What I ended up listening to amounted to a case of propositions versus a rule for living. Hang on, it's Easter, a time that's all about a rule for living; because when it comes to resurrection, we're left propositionless and in wonder. Maybe a few more meals and drinks with Jake will see both of us changed, because this guy's got stuff going on. I'll just be interested to see if Buddha will bring him the distance.

Pimps, Clients and the Soho Triangle

Protest4 is gaining momentum. The collective are working hard on putting this beer-mat campaign together for London. Our network of contacts is growing and things seem to be getting a little beyond our control. And yet, all our strategizing, planning and work to dent this trading in people hasn't made any difference to Jackie (a trafficked girl deceived into coming to the U.K. with the promise of "a better life," who has found herself in the hands of pimps and clients). Emma's been working with Jackie for a year now. There have been moments when she has looked set to walk, but the pressures and threats are too much, and so she stays.

Ironically, on the night we participate in a conference with some MPs on the issue of human trafficking, Jackie calls Emma and leaves a message: "Emma, please come and meet me if you can, I really need to talk with you." After the conference, Emma tries to make the call, but there's no response. Within days, Jackie has vanished without trace. London's Soho triangle has swallowed another girl who has been raped, lied to and broken. Emma visits the brothels and flats, desperately seeking information, with none to be found. Everyone plays ignorant, and another precious child of God

goes under. "God, where are You, and where is Jackie?"
As some of these entries might indicate, mission in London appears, on the whole, futile. And yet there is something in many of us causing us to refuse to believe that things need to stay the way they are. For too long we've seen the Body of Christ remain a bloodless abstraction; now, with our weaknesses and imperfections, we're trying to give it some flesh. God is being reborn within the systems surrounding us. In our political world, our local pubs, our neighborhoods and our churches, His "reincarnation" is taking place.

With the impossibility of such mission, our spirited collective tenacity is vital. With the disappointments of countless other Jackies, our shared hope is the only thing capable of sustaining us. With the self-doubt and too-frequent unbelief, we can only go on and, along with the poet W. S. Merwin, say, "Thanks."

> in a culture up to its chin in shame
> living in the stench it has chosen we are saying thank you.[1]

REFLECTIONS ON WORSHIP
Darrell Smith

There is something about creativity that creates space and imparts or invites relationship. There's also something about creativity that is part of being made in the image of God. Whether the artist intends it or not, his or her work often reflects the brilliance, the beauty and the radiance of God. We need to take the time to explore other cultures, other expressions, other orthodoxies, other liturgies—whatever it is that you want to try out, explore those things.

One of the coolest places I've ever worshiped God was at a plane-

tarium. We're always bringing people to our church; the space that has our gear and our setup. But can't we explore the majesty of God in other places? What if we were more thematic in our expression? If environment is so important and if nature is a key inspiration in worship, why can't we say, "We're not meeting here this morning. Grab your coats; we're going to the beach."

Does that resonate with you? The interesting thing is that when people come to worship in the church, they don't at all expect to be part of creating the environment in which they worship. People simply come and enjoy or experience the existing environment. In fact, we even borrow the words we sing because we relate to someone else's song.

In the context of worship, then, is music something that makes meeting the Creator of the Universe less awkward? Is music something that we use to sort of manage that somewhat awkward moment? When you break it down to meeting with the Creator who knows you inside and out, this is a daunting thought.

What is it about the worship environment that is conducive or intrusive to worship? Are there things about an environment that you've experienced or maybe are creating that have heightened, enhanced or somehow taken the experience of worship to a new level? Are there things that have intruded on that moment?

THE LETTER
Tim Garrety

I am a lover of "the question." As such, my blog will always be a forum for the question. While it may be deconstructive in nature, it should never be taken for granted that answers are not being pursued, that belief is not present and that conviction is not central.

REFLECT

Take a few minutes to write down your thoughts in response to the questions from Darrell Smith's worship reflections.

As I pursue Christ, I ask questions along the way and allow Him to plant answers in my soul, as opposed to drafting my answers upon my own understanding for the purpose of being spewed upon a page (or in a blog). With this said, the current manifestation of "church" has always baffled me. There is a quote by Richard Halverson that gets bludgeoned to death in many circles but is profound just the same (the version below has been edited as well):

> Christianity started out in Palestine as a fellowship. It moved to Greece and became a philosophy. Then it went to Rome and became an institution. Finally it came to America, and it became an enterprise.

It is this institutional enterprise that has, in all my 13 years of journeying with Christ, caused me perpetual head scratching. I have a good friend (in the early stages of divorce) who was sharing with me a few weeks ago that he wished his soon-to-be ex-wife would more fully understand who he is. He began to recount his past, which is littered with institutional incarceration. He lamented to me that because he had been incarcerated for longer than 90 percent of his adult life, he has become institutionalized himself. The effects of this were, among other things, an impaired ability to make good decisions. When he and I dine together, it's a running joke that he has to eat everything on his plate with a spoon. This has become deeply embedded in his behavior as a result of not having any other eating utensils in prison. It's not that he doesn't recognize the usefulness of a fork or knife or that he lacks the ability to use them. He has simply chosen to live out his limited and comfortable dining regimen. I think the intuitive reader is already catching where I'm going with this.

I need to take a bit of a rabbit trail. I am a longtime punk rock fan. From the time I was 11, I was listening to this kind of music. Even today, at 32, with a wife and a child, I can't escape my punk rock roots. One thing that has changed is that while I once bought into the idea portrayed in the music, now I find that I learn much about humanity and those whose hope does not lie with God. One of my favorite bands has been Suicidal Tendencies. The lead singer, Mike Muir, has experienced a harrowing life, to say the least. He wrote a song from his personal experience called "Institutionalized." At first blush, it reads like a teenage, angst-filled anthem against authority. However, there is much to be learned about "church," because its effects are not all that much unlike Mike Muir's musings. Here's an excerpt from the chorus of the song:

> Drug you up because they're lazy
> It's too much work to help a crazy.[2]

With that said, let's talk about "the letter." It's the tool of the institutionalized Christian. The letter is an opportunity to feel as though we have had a dialogue even though our thoughts are firmly ensconced in a medium that is purely monologue. It's interesting that even psychologists will suggest to their subjects that they write their fears, angers and frustrations, not for purposes of sharing them, but because it is a therapeutic act intended to make the writer feel better. The institutional church is interesting in that it has crushed, similar to Mike Muir's experience (although not necessarily in church), the individual's ability to think, process and commune in such a way that his or her only recourse is the one-dimensional, self-serving medium of the letter.

Let me get straight to my point. Why do we write letters to our pastors and leaders and complain about things that we've never had conversations with them about? The letter allows us to pour out our presuppositions without tempering them in the fire of conflict and relationship. Relationship and care is predicated upon the yield of conflict resolution and the free-flowing marketplace of ideas. Institutionalized Christianity has so suffocated the dimension of thought in individual practitioners that the primary vehicle for opposition is one that can't be formed through dialogue.

These letters, written to spiritual leaders, are an interesting type. They profess care, they quote Scripture, and they even cite ideals of righteousness. They rely on the Scripture, which supports the writer's neuroses and frustrations, yet they see fit to leave out the clearly scriptural mandate for communal interaction, face-to-face confrontation and reconciliation. The truth is that these letters that contain professions of care and righteousness care only about the writer and seek only to establish the writer's righteousness. What is the use of that?

GOD'S TIME
Charles Lee

When I went through seminary, I learned a lot of things about God and some great methods of research, but my theological experience didn't really prepare me philosophically to deal with a lot of things in life. I grew up in a Presbyterian church that was very reformed, and one of the primary tenets of faith was Calvinism. After seminary, I came to realize that there are elements of thinking about God in nature and time that may actually be different from what I had previously conceived. For some time, I just lived in that paradox. Now I know that there is an element of mystery about God and theology. I love that mystery, but I don't think we should settle on mystery without grappling with some of the issues involved first.

I want to throw out some questions that I get in church and in some of the classes I teach at a local college. People often ask, "Why should I be motivated about the future if it is predetermined by God? How does prayer work if the future is already determined? How do things like missions and sharing one's faith fit into this picture?"

Traditionally, when people study the Early Church fathers like Augustine, Aquinas and others, they find that this question has always been asked: If God experiences some type of duration, would it be possible for God to change? And if God can change, what does that do to our understanding of our perception of God's immutable or unchanging demeanor? That's just the root of the tension and the root of this discussion about time. Historically, people have said, "Well, God can't change; therefore, if God experiences duration and interaction, He has to be somehow outside of time. As soon as He interacts with time, what if there's an aspect of Him that changes?"

So let's ask a few more questions here: What do you think God's relationship to time might be? Have you ever thought about this? Does God have a sense of time? Is God inside of time or outside of time? If God is outside of time, are things within time predetermined?

From that vantage point, more questions come up. Let's say you get saved at age 33 and you continue to live life as a Christian until you're 80 years old. Some people have asked about this particular concept: Which part of you goes to heaven? The you before 33 or the you after 33?

REFLECT

Take a few minutes to write down your thoughts about Charles Lee's reflections on time.

I SPY

Michel Cicero

I've committed myself to seeing more light than darkness in this world.

I'm standing in front of my son Sam's school, waiting for him to be dismissed, when I notice a mother I am acquainted with approaching the crossing guard. The mother lives with her daughter in the Avenue area and they ride the bus to and from school every day. The mother always walks her daughter from the bus stop to her classroom, and then walks a pretty good distance home. Every day. They are not well off financially, and it would appear that the mother is a little edgy. It would *appear*. I've always been in awe of the love that enables this woman to ride public transportation round trip twice, every day of the week, rather than make her daughter do it alone.

The crossing guard is elderly and often irritable. I love her because she escorts my son across the street safely twice daily, but I've never gone deeper with her than, "Hi, how are you today?" or "Yeah, it's cold, isn't it?" I don't know why I haven't gone deeper, I just haven't.

So there I am, waiting for Sam, who is quite late, when God allows me to be privy to a shared moment between the mother and the elderly woman. The mother approaches the woman with a crocheted blanket. It has been uncommonly cold for a week or so, and anyone willing to see the crossing guard would realize that she must be pretty cold sitting all day outside on her folding beach chair. This hadn't occurred to me, but it obviously occurred to the bus-riding mother. The crossing guard accepted the blanket, the two hugged, and the mother left.

There was something so intentional about this event and my witnessing of it. I think God presents me with moments such as these to confirm that He's near and present in people and situations everywhere.

A DOUBT EMBRACED BY FAITH

Charles Lee

Plunged into open waters
Surrendered to uncertainty
Permeated by forbidden fruit
A Doubt Embraced by Faith

Misunderstood by the established
Packaged with emergent
Labeled by the labeled
Wearied by angst
A Doubt Embraced by Faith

Life as an independent film
Clashing metaphors
Unresolved melodies
Overwhelmed by futility
Comforted by sorrow
A Doubt Embraced by Faith

Invited to question
Intrigued by mystery
Wooed by tension

A paradoxical wonder
Abandoned to trust
In search for sacred space
A Doubt Embraced by Faith

REFLECT

Add your own journalings of your adventure as a practitioner.

NOTES

1. W. S. Merwin, "Thanks," *The Rain in the Trees* (New York: Knopf, 1988), n.p.
   E. Glenn Wagner, *The Awesome Power of Shared Beliefs* (Dallas: Word Publishing, 1995), n.p.
2. Mike Muir, "Institutionalized," *Suicidal Tendencies*, © 1983.

ABOUT THE EDITORS

Greg Russinger

Greg is married to Michele, and they share life, love and laughter with their daughter, Ashtin, and their son, Liam. Greg lives out his faith with a people known as The Bridge Community in Ventura, California. Their collective efforts and hopes include the Soliton Network and Sessions, a local and global friendship of curious and imaginative practitioners of faith, justice and mission; and Oneorphan, a global advocacy effort for the poor and the orphan. You will usually find Greg walking the sidewalks of the city or sitting and reading a book or tucked away in a movie theater dreaming the dreams of God.

Alex Field

Alex Field is a freelance writer and the author of the book *The Hollywood Project*. He has written for the *Los Angeles Times*, *RES Magazine*, *Relevant Magazine* and *Outreach Magazine*. He is an editor for Gospel Light in Southern California, where he lives with his wife, Nicole, and sons, Ari and Elijah.

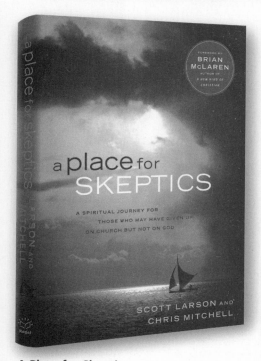

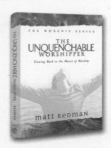

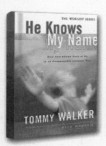

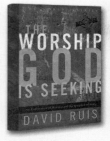